LETA STETTER HOLLINGWORTH

LETA STETTER HOLLINGWORTH

LETA STETTER HOLLINGWORTH

A BIOGRAPHY

BY

Harry L. Hollingworth

WITH A FOREWORD BY

Ludy T. Benjamin, Jr.
Texas A&M University

AND

Stephanie A. Shields
University of California, Davis

ANKER PUBLISHING COMPANY
Bolton, MA

LETA STETTER HOLLINGWORTH:
A Biography

Copyright © 1990 by Anker Publishing Company. All rights reserved. Printed in the United States of America. Except as permitted under the United States Copyright Act of 1976, no part of this publication may be reproduced or distributed in any form or by any means, or stored in a data base or retrieval system, without the prior written permission of the publisher.

Anker Publishing Company
176 Ballville Road
P.O. Box 249
Bolton, MA 01740

ISBN 0-9627042-0-2

Original edition was published by the University of Nebraska Press in 1943.

Another came and stood within the place
Where softly breathing lay the living snow,
And looked upon the waste and bending low,
Stooped as he loved it. Then I saw his face!
He gathered all the petals at his feet
And thro his life they gave him fragrance sweet.

                        Leta A. Stetter, 1906

Contents

Foreword   ix

1	Introduction	1
2	Ancestry	5
3	Birth and Infancy	15
4	Childhood	23
5	High-School Days	31
6	College Years	39
7	Life Plans	47
8	A High-School Teacher	54
9	Attitudes and Viewpoints	59
10	Feelings and Emotions	67
11	An Interlude and Marriage	72
12	Clinical Psychology Begins	75
13	A Doctor of Philosophy	79
14	Poems Written in Adult Life	81

15	Early Research and Publications	85
16	A Home at Last	93
17	At Teachers College, Columbia University	99
18	Courses of Instruction and Books	103
19	First Educational Experiment	113
20	The Special Opportunity Class (P. S. 165)	116
21	A Tour of Inspection Abroad	122
22	At Public School 500 (Speyer School)	126
23	A Doctor of Laws	135
24	Interests of Leta S. Hollingworth	138
25	Personal and Home Life	145
26	The Memorial Conference	152

Bibliography   159

Foreword*

In the early 1970s, we were among a small number of psychologists who went looking for the historical roots of the psychology of women and discovered the pioneering work of Leta Stetter Hollingworth (1886–1939). Independently, we published articles on Hollingworth's legacy in 1975, the International Women's Year. In the 15 years since that time there has been considerable attention devoted to Hollingworth as psychologist, educator, and feminist, resulting in a number of publications about her life and work. A bibliography of this recent scholarship and older articles appears at the end of this book.

This re-discovery of Leta Hollingworth has focused on three areas in which she made significant contributions: a) the psychology of women and sex differences, b) clinical psychology, and c) educational psychology, particularly education of the gifted child. We would like to summarize those contributions.

Psychology of Women and Sex Differences

Hollingworth began her graduate work at Columbia University's Teachers College where she decided to look critically at the status of women. Claims for the intellectual inferiority of women were in many published scientific works, yet her reading revealed no scientific data to support these claims. One claim was that "women, by virtue of their menstrual

---

*Portions of this foreword are taken from our chapter in *Women in Psychology*, A. N. O'Connell and N. F. Russo, Eds. (Greenwood Press, Westport, CT, 1990). Copyright © by Agnes N. O'Connell and Nancy Felipe Russo. We are grateful to the editors and Greenwood Press for permission to use this material.

functions, experience regularly recurring interferences with the use of all their abilities, and must be considered for a considerable part of each lunar period as invalids, or semi invalids" (Hollingworth, 1943, p. 114). That topic would be the subject of her dissertation research, for which she received a Ph.D. in 1916.

Of more immediate concern to her was the variability hypothesis: The assertion that "Women as a species are less variable among themselves than are men; all women are pretty much alike but men range enormously in their talents and defects" (Hollingworth, 1943, p. 114). The variability hypothesis (see Shields, 1982) flourished in the early 1900s principally through armchair dogma in the literature of psychology, education, medicine, and sociology. This hypothesis was used to explain the greater frequency of men on lists of distinction as well as their greater number on lists of immorality and criminality. It was also used to explain a wider range of intelligence for men—more male geniuses, but also more institutionalized males. At the time she began to work with him, Leta Hollingworth's major professor, Edward L. Thorndike, was a proponent of the variability hypothesis.

After receiving her M.A. and a Master's Diploma in Education in 1913, Hollingworth continued her graduate studies supported by work at the Clearing House for Mental Defectives where she was employed to administer Binet tests. Placing her faith in data rather than dogma, she designed several ingenious studies to examine the relation between social factors and the comparative variability of the sexes. In order to minimize the effects of environment on physical variability she and Helen Montague measured physical characteristics of 2000 neonates. Suffice it to say, they found no sex-related difference in variability on any measure (Montague & Hollingworth, 1914a). Comparing age at admission and sex ratios in institutions for the "feebleminded," she found an interesting bias in those data: as the age of admission increased, the proportion of female to male admissions increased (Hollingworth, 1914a; 1922). She concluded that

> The boy who cannot compete mentally is found out, becomes at an early age an object of concern to relatives, is brought to the Clearing-House and directed toward an institution. The girl who cannot compete mentally is not so often recognized as definitely defective, since it is not unnatural for her to drop into the isolation of the home, where she can "take care of" small children, peel po-

tatoes, scrub, etc. ... Thus they survive outside of institutions. (Hollingworth, 1914a, pp. 515–516).

Hollingworth persistently argued that a fundamental reexamination of women's social role in industrial society was needed. The crux of the problem was obvious to her: Women bear children and, for centuries, had been trained to, expected to, and if need be, coerced to devote themselves to the care of their offspring (Hollingworth, 1916a). Women's many and varied talents had traditionally been channeled away from social achievement and into childrearing and housekeeping, fields "where eminence is impossible" (Hollingworth, 1914a, p.526). Or, as she noted elsewhere, "No one knows who is the best housekeeper in America. Eminent housekeepers do not and cannot exist" (Hollingworth, 1940, p. 16). Careful to caution that her criticism of law and social convention should not be "construed as an attack on maternity," she emphasized that the real problem was "a social order that has been built up on the assumption that there is and can be little or no variation in tastes, interests, and abilities within the female sex" (1914a, pp. 526 and 528; see also 1916b, 1918, 1927, 1928). To make her point clearly, she relied on a simple thought experiment. She asked the reader to

> Imagine a man and a woman of exactly equal ability, allowed to compete intellectually for a given social prize, on the condition that each shall become the parent of two or three children. Under the prevailing economic and social order, there is no question as to which will win. (1916c, p. 933).

She believed that scientific study of the important issues facing women was essential to overcome the custom of bias that hampered much-needed social change. In the meantime, each woman who deviated from the norms of the accepted role was faced with unique problems and was forced to produce unique solutions to them. It was the sum of these "experimental lives" (her choice of words is noteworthy given the high value she placed on scientific data) that would eventually produce new, broader, and more suitable guidelines for the courses that a woman's life could take.

Leta Hollingworth's actual research on the psychology of women ended shortly after she received her doctoral degree, but her interest in these issues continued throughout her life. According to Harry Hollingworth (1943), his wife had long planned a book on the social psychology of women titled *Mrs. Pilgrim's Progress*. Leta Hollingworth's work was among the first to challenge scientifically the assertions of the biological inferiority of women. Hollingworth's data and arguments against the variability hypothesis and for a consideration of social factors did not miraculously change psychological theory, but did have an impact on several influential individuals. By the 1920s Edward Thorndike no longer referred to the variability hypothesis as either a potent discriminator between the abilities of women and men or as an explanatory concept. Somewhat later, Lewis Terman began to allow that social discrimination may be an important impediment to women's intellectual and social achievement. During her life Hollingworth was hailed as the "scientific pillar" of the women's movement and today her work is well known among psychologists who study the social psychology of gender.

Clinical Psychology

When Leta Hollingworth was hired at the Clearing House in 1913, she took the position as a temporary replacement for Emily T. Burr, one of the earliest workers in the field. Leta Hollingworth was kept on with Burr after her return. In 1914 the psychological examiners giving mental tests were put under Civil Service supervision, and after competitive exams Hollingworth was at the top of the list. The first opening was at Bellevue Hospital. Later she was offered the position of chief of a psychological lab to be established at the hospital. At about this time she completed the Ph.D. and was offered the late Naomi Norsworthy's position in educational psychology at Columbia's Teachers College (see Higgins, 1918) which she "reluctantly" accepted (Hollingworth, 1943). She remained in that position for the rest of her life: She was promoted from instructor to Assistant Professor in 1919, to Associate Professor in 1922, and to Professor in 1929.

She continued part-time work as a clinical psychologist until 1920. "Clinical psychology" was, at that time, a grab-bag term applied primarily to the field of mental testing. Her job was to test "mentally inferior" individuals for commitment by the courts. She was active in the controversy surrounding who was properly fitted to give and interpret psychological tests and was a leader in the move to build professionalism and raise the standards of mental examiners in universities and in the Civil Service (Poffenberger, 1940). During this period her research centered upon the characteristics of mental deficiency and of special mental disabilities. Her research in this area appeared in two books, *The Psychology of Subnormal Children* (1920) and *Special Talents and Defects* (1923). In working with these "mentally defective" children she soon realized that many of them were of normal intelligence but suffered from emotional and attitudinal problems due to adjustment difficulties especially during adolescence, so she began to focus more directly on that age group (Poffenberger, 1940). She developed courses on Mental Adjustments and Adolescence and published *The Psychology of the Adolescent* (1928). The book became a standard in the field for the next two decades.

A particularly good example of Leta Hollingworth's activism can be found in her efforts to professionalize clinical psychologists. World War I had given tremendous impetus to the testing movement and clinical psychology and during the post-war years there was an increasing demand for psychologists in all areas of industry and education. In the American Psychological Association (APA), which had repeatedly raised its requirements for membership, nearly half of the 300-plus members were involved in some type of applied work. Many involved in applied work believed that the organization did not meet their professional needs. The APA had done little toward establishing standards for practitioners and, in general, seemed to have no interest in psychology outside of the academy. The first organized effort of applied psychologists to correct this situation came in 1917 at the annual meeting when a group of clinical psychologists, headed by Leta Hollingworth, attempted to form an independent professional organization, the American Association of Clinical Psychology. Argument and controversy postponed action and the following year APA did set up a committee to consider certification of "consulting psychologists" and to establish a Clinical Section within APA.

Educational Psychology and the Gifted Child

In her capacity as a clinical psychologist, Hollingworth became more and more frequently asked to help out with mentally gifted children who were experiencing educational or emotional problems. Most psychologists and educators of her day were of the opinion that 'the bright can take care of themselves.' It was in this field that she established her reputation on an international basis. In the 1920s there were fewer than a half-dozen individuals doing research on gifted education. Her work with a seven-year-old boy who was placed in the fifth grade, but who was still insufficiently challenged, led her to meet Jacob Theobald, then a school principal (PS 165) and later a member of the Board of Superintendents of New York City. Their consideration of the particular problems of this boy ultimately led to her first experiment with the gifted.

Hollingworth worked intensively with gifted children in two major projects. One of her Ph.D. students, Miriam Pritchard (Pritchard, 1951), has described these two educational experiments in detail in her summary of Hollingworth's contributions to the study of the gifted. During the course of each project Hollingworth observed the children almost every school day. She maintained contact with the children in her first experimental group for the rest of her life. She repeatedly emphasized the importance of identifying gifted children early in life, believing that these children could greatly benefit from supplemental educational experience. She believed that it was children at the extremes of intelligence who most needed ability grouping because it was at the extremes that the regular school structure failed to meet the individual child's needs. In the rest of the child's life she thought exceptional children should not be isolated from other children.

The first of her educational experiments began in 1922 with the formation of two Special Opportunity classes at PS 165. The children, identified through a city-wide search were 7 to 9 years old when the special classes were established. The special classes were continued for three years. During the experiment, and even in the years after they graduated, she studied all aspects of the children's lives, including gifted children's size and strength, sibling relations, musical sensitivity, play behavior, and personality characteristics. *Gifted Children* (1926) described some of this work, and like her book on adolescence, it served as a standard reference work in schools of education for many years.

Her second experiment involved children at a specially-established school, Speyer School (PS 500), to study the special educational problems of the slow learner and of the gifted learner. Leta Hollingworth was the advisor for the two gifted classes and W.B. Featherstone the advisor for the two slow learner classes. The goal was to optimize learning for the individual limits and talents of the child. Hollingworth, adopting the philosophy of her graduate school mentor, E.L. Thorndike, believed that the education of the best thinkers should be an "education for initiative and originality," and so not just an accelerated version of the normal curriculum, but a program specially geared to help these children develop attitudes, understandings, appreciations, which would enhance their childhood and help them become more effective adults (Pritchard, 1951).

She was also quite interested in the exceptionally gifted child who tests at greater than IQ 180. Her interest in high intelligence first was stimulated by a demonstration of individual testing that she conducted for one of her classes in 1916. The child, who had been recommended to her as exceptional, achieved the impressive IQ of 187. She continued to follow Child E—'s development to adulthood (Garrison, Burke, & Hollingworth, 1917; Hollingworth, Garrison, & Burke, 1922; Hollingworth, 1927). Her book, *Children Above 180 I.Q.* (1942), which was completed by her husband after her death, summarizes her longitudinal study of 12 exceptionally gifted individuals. Among the things she found out about these exceptionally gifted children was that many of them, from the time of their entry into school, experienced adjustment problems because of inept treatment by adults and lack of intellectual challenge. Hollingworth's work did much to dispel the notion that very bright children are fragile, clumsy, and eccentric.

Leta Hollingworth's concern with righting wrongs is especially evident in her writing on education late in her career. She was disturbed by the false egalitarianism of American education that refused to acknowledge individual differences in intellectual capacity and make allowances for them in children's education. One recurrent theme in her commentaries on education is that by enforcing rigid programs, education had succeeded only in ensuring widespread mediocrity resulting in a loss of talent that would inevitably have negative consequences for society. She believed that, overall, IQ tests were the most equitable means of identifying highly gifted children (and given the alternatives in the 1930s, she was probably right). She argued that assertions about race differences in intelligence had not been objectively or adequately studied to support any conclusion and, in reprising her earlier observations regarding sex differences, that the social context of development must be an acknowledged factor in any such research. If science could develop ways of identifying the child who would become the high-achieving adult "we should then be able to select and cherish human genius without regard to race, sex or condition of economic servitude" (Garrison, Burke, & Hollingworth, 1917, pp. 102–103). Hollingworth was particularly concerned with the needs of families who could not afford to support the education of their gifted children. She frequently approached foundations and philanthropic agencies with proposals to set up scholarship funds, but the prevailing belief was that bright children would succeed on their own. Pritchard (1951) suggested that one memorandum to the American Council on Education written shortly before Hollingworth's death finally stimulated a national conference which paved the way for recommendations regarding federal scholarship support.

Leta Hollingworth was only 53 years old when abdominal cancer ended her life on November 27, 1939. Her accomplishments belie the fact that she was professionally active for less than half of that abbreviated life span. The boundaries that she battled in the search for equality of opportunity for women and education for gifted children are still boundaries today. However, they are far less formidable in contemporary society, a fact that is surely due in some measure to the force of her work.

The Biography of Leta Hollingworth

In 1908, Leta Stetter had married her University of Nebraska classmate, Harry Levi Hollingworth, who was at that time completing his doctoral work in psychology at Columbia University. Harry Hollingworth was himself a distinguished applied psychologist and served as president of APA in 1927. He and Leta enjoyed a close relationship and he was very supportive of her efforts throughout her career. After her death he published her public addresses and a collection of her poetry (1940), and in 1943 he wrote her biography, the only full-length biography of Leta Hollingworth to date. It was published by the University of Nebraska Press in 1943.

Due to shortages of paper during the second world war, the federal government established guidelines that restricted publication. Thus only a small number of copies of this book were published. It has long been out of print and would-be readers have had difficulty locating a copy.

Due to the rediscovery of Leta Hollingworth's work by scholars working in psychology, gifted education, and women's studies, this biography has acquired new significance. We are grateful that Anker Publishing Company has reissued this book and hope that its availability will introduce this and subsequent generations to the significant accomplishments of this remarkable woman.

We are pleased to announce that all royalties from the sale of this book will be donated to the Carolyn Wood Sherif Memorial Lectureship Fund of the American Psychological Association's Division on the Psychology of Women.

Ludy T. Benjamin, Jr.
Stephanie A. Shields

References

Garrison, C. G., Burke, A., & Hollingworth, L.S. (1917). The psychology of a prodigious child. *Journal of Applied Psychology, 1,* 101–110.

Higgins, F.C. (1918). *The life of Naomi Norsworthy.* NY: Houghton Mifflin.

Hollingworth, H. L. (1943). *Leta Stetter Hollingworth.* Lincoln, NE: University of Nebraska Press.

Hollingworth, L. S. (1913). The frequency of amentia as related to sex. *Medical Record, 84,* 753–756.

Hollingworth, L. S. (1914a). Variability as related to sex differences in achievement. *American Journal of Sociology, 19,* 510–530.

Hollingworth, L. S. (1914b). Functional periodicity. *Teachers College Contributions to Education,* No. 69, NY: Columbia University Press.

Hollingworth, L. S. (1916a). Social devices for impelling women to bear and rear children. *American Journal of Sociology, 22,* 19–29.

Hollingworth, L. S. (1916b). The vocational aptitudes of women. In H. L. Hollingworth (Ed.), *Vocational Psychology,* (pp. 222-244). NY: D. Appleton.

Hollingworth, L. S. (1916c). Phi Beta Kappa and women students. *School and Society, 4,* 932–933.

Hollingworth, L. S. (1918). Comparison of the sexes in mental traits. *Psychological Bulletin, 15,* 427–432.

Hollingworth, L. S. (1920). *The psychology of subnormal children.* NY: Macmillan.

Hollingworth, L. S. (1922). Differential action upon the sexes of forces which tend to segregate the feeble-minded. *Journal of Abnormal and Social Psychology, 17,* 35–57.

Hollingworth, L. S. (1923). *Special talents and defects: Their significance for education.* NY: Macmillan.

Hollingworth, L. S. (1926). *Gifted children.* NY: Macmillan.

Hollingworth, L. S. (1927). Subsequent history of E—: Ten years after the initial report. *Journal of Applied Psychology, 11,* 385–390.

Hollingworth, L. S. (1927, October). The new woman in the making. *Current History, 27,* 15–20.

Hollingworth, L. S. (1928). *The psychology of the adolescent.* NY: D. Appleton.

Hollingworth, L. S. (1940). *Public addresses.* Lancaster, PA: Science Press.

Hollingworth, L. S. (1942). *Children above 180 I.Q.* Yonkers, NY: World Book Company.

Hollingworth, L. S., Garrison, C.G., & Burke, A. (1922). Subsequent history of E———: Five years after the initial report. *Journal of Applied Psychology, 6,* 205–210.

Montague, H., & Hollingworth, L. S. (1914). The comparative variability of the sexes at birth. *American Journal of Sociology, 20,* 335–370.

Poffenberger, A. T. (1940). Leta Stetter Hollingworth: 1886–1939. *American Journal of Psychology, 53,* 299–301.

Pritchard, M. C. (1951). The contributions of Leta S. Hollingworth to the study of gifted children. In P. Witty (Ed.), *The gifted child,* Chapter 4. Boston: D.C. Heath.

Shields, S. A. (1982). The variability hypothesis. *Signs, 7,* 769–797.

1

Introduction

Sixty years ago what is now Dawes County, Nebraska, a fairly prosperous cattle raising section of the state, was an unoccupied sandhill waste. The Sioux Indians roved over it, and later were corralled in the Rosebud and Pine Ridge reservations. No railroad ran through that section of Nebraska, but what is now the Northwestern was being built out in that direction. The section from O'Neill to Valentine was worked on especially at that time.

The sandhills stretched for miles in any direction. There were only occasional and small streams, such as the White River, flowing weakly enough between crumbling banks and gradually washing out deep gullies. Here and there were unexpected bluffs and gorges, some of them wild and picturesque. There were no trees except a few cottonwoods along the streams. To the north lay the Black Hills and the Bad Lands. To the south was a vast and relatively unfrequented stretch of the state of Nebraska, mainly desert.

The buffalo had gone but the ground bore a covering of tough grass which, if the acreage were large enough, made adequate grazing for cattle. The territory still afforded good hunting and trapping. It had been free range land but was being offered now for homesteading. Tenant farmers and younger sons from Ohio and Illinois especially were being encouraged to move in along the new rail route, and to plow up the range land. They confidently hoped to imitate the bumper crops of their home states, to which in turn most of them had come or been brought from Kentucky, Virginia and Tennessee.

It required a good half-century to teach these migrants, or their children, that drouth and grasshoppers were too great and too inevitable a handicap for such agricultural enterprise. Confidently they excavated dugouts for temporary dwellings or built sod houses for longer use. As materials could be found, and after the railroad came through, as it did in time, log houses and frame shanties supplanted these more primitive shelters. Year after year they plowed up ever more sod and grazing land, and fenced it off. They planted more rows of corn, more oats and wheat. As land grew somewhat in speculative value and settlers increased in number, moneylenders appeared. It became possible to mortgage the homestead and thus to ensure a few more years of baffled defeat.

On May 25, 1886, in a dugout on the White River, five or six miles from the site of what is now Chadron, Nebraska, Leta Anna Stetter was born to the daughter of such a migrant farmer and his wife. The farmer was also a preacher; they had not long ago arrived there and had burrowed in, full of hope and faith in the provident guidance of a Presbyterian deity.

As she grew to childhood, Leta Stetter went to a little log schoolhouse that the settlers had built. In due time she finished high school in Valentine, Nebraska, in a neighboring county. Thence she went to the University of Nebraska, at Lincoln, the state capital, from which institution she was graduated in the Class of 1906 with the highest honors.

After teaching in high schools in the state for two or three years she reversed the trail of her migrant west-bound ancestors and went east to New York City. She married there a former classmate at the University of Nebraska and continued in graduate and professional study.

In due course she received the degrees of M.A. and Ph.D. from Columbia University, and began pioneer work as a clinical psychologist in the schools and hospitals of New York City. Striking out along many lines of scholarship, she speedily achieved professional and scientific distinction, and became well known for her contributions to the literature of education. She became first Instructor and finally full Professor of Education in Teachers College, Columbia University, in a day when few women were accorded such opportunity. She attained international influence in her chosen fields, becoming the author of half a dozen authoritative volumes and nearly a hundred technical and popular papers and articles in journals devoted to education, psychology, and social science.

Accounts of her and her work were included in many cyclopedias of well-known people, such as *Who's Who in America, Who's Who in the East, Who's Who in Education, Who's Who in Literature, American Men of Science, Women of Achievement,* and others. After receiving various honors and citations for her work in the East, she was given in 1937 the honorary degree of Doctor of Laws (LL.D.) by her Alma Mater, the University of Nebraska. On that occasion the same degree was conferred on her husband. Simultaneous honorary degrees are not often bestowed on two members of the same family. For thirty years they had worked together in related fields and in the same eastern university.

This volume is devoted to an account of the life and work of Leta Stetter Hollingworth, who was often fondly referred to by people who knew her history as "the first white child born in Dawes County, Nebraska." At the same time it gives an incidental picture of a period not too often described—the rather stodgy agricultural quarter-century sandwiched in between the "sod house frontier" and the "machine age" in the Middle West.

It has been difficult to secure accurate information on the earlier years of her life, and especially on her forbears. No systematic records are available, and most of those who might remember the facts are gone or are inaccessible. There are no diaries to throw light on the earlier period of her life. For the most part the account of these years is based on her oral communications during her lifetime, on her personal letters to the writer over a third of a century of acquaintance and mutual interest, and on a few brief memoranda found among her papers, or provided by relatives.

Leta Stetter Hollingworth died at 6:05 P.M. on November 27, 1939, in the Presbyterian Hospital, Medical Center, New York City, after an acute illness of six weeks. She rests in a spot chosen by herself only a few months before her death in Wyuka Cemetery, Lincoln, Nebraska.

In a "home-coming letter" written by her on December 3, 1937, to the editor of *The Nebraska State Journal,* she said:

> One more thing I would say. Sometime I shall come back to Nebraska for good. I was born there. I was reared there. I was educated there. I shall take the last long sleep there. The East is too alien for purposes of eternal sleep.

Information concerning the last thirty years of her life and activities is easily enough available, so far as objective aspects are concerned. This information is to be found in scholarly records, in papers, books, memoranda, and other reports of her work as an educator and scientist.

The very earliest period of her life is recorded in a little manuscript left by her mother, describing the events of the first year of life of her eldest daughter. It is the period of childhood and adolescence, and the very earliest years of her maturity, for which no such records are to be found. In order to make this account not wholly dependent for its veridity on my personal recollection and opinions, I have endeavored to exhibit, as well as may be, the array of her interests, her attitudes and feelings, and to some extent her more objective activities, by selected quotations from some of her letters.

Leta Stetter Hollingworth wrote many letters. On a conservative estimate she wrote at least a thousand letters a year for a period of thirty years. Most of these are scattered over the face of the earth, and in the most varied hands. But several hundred of them were addressed to me and these are the only ones I have made use of.

No complete letter is given here; all the more personal features, and all comments on our own relationships have been omitted; details dealing with current events and the like are also eliminated. Only special sections of a few letters are chosen, that they may as clearly as possible reveal the personality of the writer in her youth, and for the sake of whatever light they may be able to throw on her childhood, of which the records are so fragmentary.

It is in some respects a pity that the world at large could not be admitted more freely to the letters and other personal communications of Leta Stetter Hollingworth. They are so full of zest, so marked by eagerness for experience and knowledge, so characterized by serious purpose and wise insight, with a constant undertone of merriment and tenderness, so free and facile in their expression, that many people would find in them a source of deep pleasure. A colleague, writing in the *Teachers College Record* on the occasion of her death, had seen enough of her communications to have caught their spirit, and he said, "A social letter from her was likely to be a gem worthy of a gilt frame and a place among one's literary treasures." But no further exhibition of her letters shall be made; they are used here, even in fragments, only because they are the sole surviving objective records of her personality and experience during the period of her life to which they relate.

2

Ancestry

GREAT-GRANDPARENTS

In Clark County, Kentucky, on April 4, 1803, a son was born to Samuel Danley and his wife Elizabeth Danley. The father, of Irish descent, "was probably born in Kentucky." The mother, of Scottish descent, was born in Virginia. This son was named Levi Danley. In turn he married Margaret McClure, and to them were born seven sons and one daughter. One of these sons, Samuel Thomas Danley, married, on September 14, 1859, Mary Ellen Blair. This couple had two children, William A. Danley and Margaret Elinor Danley. The daughter, Margaret Elinor, who was born April 1, 1862, married John G. Stetter in or near Chadron, Nebraska, and became the mother, on May 25, 1886, of Leta Anna Stetter, to whose life and career this volume is devoted.

This brief statement spans five generations. On the Danley and Blair side there are records available in some detail of the activities and characteristics of the ancestry of Leta Stetter Hollingworth. On her father's side much less information is at hand. Although it is far from clear how much influence the characteristics of particular relatives may have on the make-up and destiny of an individual, it is commonly felt that an account of one's forbears gives at least an instructive background for the picture of a personality, however great the resemblances or differences disclosed. Therefore such facts as are available concerning these earlier generations will be here set forth, beginning with the great-grandparents on the maternal side.

A sketch of Levi Danley is included in "The Old Settlers of McLean County," edited June 1, 1874, at which time the subject of the sketch was seventy-one years old. He did not die, however, until the fall of

1900, at the age of ninety-seven. At this date his great-granddaughter, Leta Stetter, was already fourteen years of age, and halfway through high school in Valentine, Nebraska.

This span of life from 1803 to 1900 covers a good deal of the important history of our country. In their own way Levi Danley and his descendants played active roles in this history, especially in what has been called "the winning of the West." The first thing recorded of this family relates to its movements westward. Generation after generation they followed the receding frontier, taking up new land and breaking the sod. Leta Stetter was herself the first one of her family to play the role of "back trailer." She, in turn, moved eastward instead, to wrestle with a very different frontier, an intellectual one, on the eastern seaboard from which her ancestors had migrated.

Of Levi Danley we are told that in boyhood he moved, with his father's family, to Fleming County, Kentucky, where he lived until he was fourteen years old. The country was "rough and sparsely settled." There was only a little schooling available, but it is recorded that Levi was "a pretty attentive scholar." In the fall of 1817 the family moved on into Illinois. Leta Stetter in her own brief autobiography wrote that "both the Danleys and the Blairs left Kentucky before the Civil War because they were abolitionists."

The family made this hard journey by four-horse team, bringing their livestock with them. They crossed the Ohio at Shawneetown and first settled "on Shoal Creek, about 9 miles west of Carlisle." In the second or third spring thereafter they moved on "into what is now Sangamon County," where they constructed "a pole camp, covered with elm bark like an Indian wigwam."

In 1827 the Black Hawk Indians threatened trouble. Levi Danley, aged twenty-four by this time, volunteered and enlisted "in a body of men commanded by Colonel Neal of Springfield." (A cousin of Leta Stetter, four generations later, bears the name of Neal Danley.) Galena, Illinois, was the headquarters of this troop. When the Indian scare was over for the time being the company returned home. Levi Danley expressed his disapproval of Galena, in that day. He reported it to be "almost as hard a place as Sodom and Gommorah, for the principal occupation of the people was gambling and drinking."

Young Levi Danley is reported to have seen many Indians and often to have "traded, ran foot races and wrestled with them." He lived in Sangamon County until February, 1829, and meantime, in 1827 he married Margaret McClure of Stout's Grove. Early in 1829, at the age of twenty-six, he and his wife moved to Stout's Grove "in what is now McLean but then was Tazewell County." The name of the town of Stout's Grove was subsequently changed to Danvers. During these years he was an ardent and successful hunter, as well as a provident farmer.

In 1832 the Black Hawk War actually broke out in earnest and Danley enlisted in another company, of which Robert McClure was Captain and John H. S. Rhodes First Lieutenant. Danley, by this time twenty-nine years old, had many stirring and sometimes gruesome adventures in this Indian warfare. The account of him asserts that "Mr. Danley has led the life of a hard working farmer and has had no particular adventures since the Black Hawk War."

He is described as "little more than five feet in height, but the one of most interest here. He was born December 14, 1833, in Illinois; he died in Rocky Ford, Colorado, in 1898. On September 14, 1859, he married Mary Ellen Blair, who was born December 14, 1838, and died July 29, 1904. It was this couple who became the grandparents of Leta Stetter Hollingworth. She always referred to them as "Grandpa and Grandma Danley." Not only did they become her grandparents, but they took her and her two younger sisters upon the mother's death, and cared for them during all their early childhood. Of them Leta Stetter Hollingworth wrote in her brief autobiography:

> My maternal grandparents are of primary importance in any biographical sketch of me, because my mother died when I was three years old, and they "raised" me and my two sisters. They were Scotch-Irish Presbyterians, and we were reared accordingly. My mother, Margaret Elinor Stetter, was their only daughter.

The Blairs are a large and notable family, or group of families, so numerous that several genealogical volumes have been devoted to them. So far as America is concerned, at least, there seem to have been several strains, coming to this country at about the same time. Two Blairs are said to have arrived in America in 1720. David, a Scot, came by way of North Ireland and settled with his group around Boston and Worcester, Massachusetts. His grandsons were old enough to fight in the Revolution. But there is no evidence that Mary Ellen Blair came from this strain.

There was a Reverend John Blair, also born in Scotland, who too arrived in America in 1720. He was a professor of divinity and was at one time associated with Princeton University. His sons, James and John, went to Kentucky and Virginia. The Kentucky branch of the family originated with James, who was a lawyer in Frankfort. The Blairs of this group have a distinguished place in our history. It would seem most probable that Mary Ellen Blair came from this line but that her family left Kentucky and migrated to Illinois. A letter from an aunt, by marriage, of Leta Stetter, written March 23, 1920, says:

> Your great-grandfather, Matthew Ralston Blair, married Eleanor Grey in Kentucky; they moved to central Illinois, had twelve children, of which your grandmother Mary was about the third, I think.

The family motto of one line of Blairs is said to have been *"Test All Things,"* or, as Leta Stetter Hollingworth was fond of rendering it, *"I love to test."* In view of her activities as a clinical psychologist, much occupied with mental testing, and as an experimenter in the field of education, she was much intrigued by this motto, and by the mortar and pestle which was said to be part of a Blair coat of arms.

A brief account of the life of Samuel Danley and his wife has been recorded in an unpublished memorandum by his son, William A. Danley of Chadron, Nebraska.

> My father, Samuel Thomas (Danley), was born in the old Danley homestead December 14, 1833. He spent his early life on the farm, afterwards attending school at Lebanon, Tennessee, preparing himself for the ministry. But his eyes failed him, and he went back to the farm.
> I was born on the old Danley homestead in the same house in which my father was born. Maggie, my sister, was born on what was known as the Roop farm, four miles further up the grove, one mile from my grandfather Blair's home.
> As I remember we lived several years on a farm three miles southwest of Danvers, afterwards buying and building a new home one mile north of Danvers. In 1873 we moved to Carthage, Missouri, where we lived one year, then going back to Danvers lived one year on the old Danley homestead.
> We then moved to Princeton, Illinois, where Maggie and I attended the High School. In 1879 we came to Niobrara, Nebraska, staying there until 1881. We then spent two years in camps grading the railroad from O'Neill to Valentine.
> In June, 1884, we came to where now stands Chadron, Nebraska, taking up a homestead near Dakota Junction. There Maggie married John G. Stetter and there Leta and Ruth were born, Maggie being born in Chadron, in the first house north of the Congregational church, where Maggie (the mother) died the day following Maggie's birth in 1892 (?).

Samuel T. Danley and Mary Ellen Blair thus led a wandering life. In part this was occasioned, as I have been told orally, by some financial chicanery of a brother, which the devout Samuel made good at the cost of all his worldly goods. He then began his migration westward from Illinois, now preaching and now farming, and doing all sorts of jobs mainly in connection with the building of the Northwestern Railroad through northern Nebraska.

Leta Stetter Hollingworth told many stories of the patient industry of this perennially defeated homesteader, and of his steady faith in the future. Yearly he plowed and sowed. Either drouth came and the corn shrivelled, or if it prospered in the early spring, then the grasshoppers swarmed over the crop, leaving only ruin behind. The sandhills, which should never have been disturbed by the plow but left as range for grazing, still seemed to be good land, if only rain would come. Hoping and praying for rain, the old preacher-farmer could only borrow on his land to put in another crop next year.

In spite of his poverty, he and his wife took to raise and support the three little granddaughters, when Maggie, their only daughter, died and left them. The children did all they could to help. They might gather the pumpkins to cut up for the cow; or carry the oats to the horses; or pull the catch on the corn-seeder that released the kernels at proper intervals while grandfather drove the team.

At first they lived in a dugout, and in such a place Leta was born. Later they built a "soddy" and still later attained the dignity of a log cabin. The children attended a log schoolhouse, played along the banks of White River, a small stream in the vicinity, and their chief toys were the natural objects that the prairie afforded. Their clothing was plain and simple enough; their underwear was often made of old flour sacks and Leta always related with pleasure the way in which she first learned to read: by deciphering the lines printed in large type on these garments, such lines as CHADRON ROLLER MILLS.

For nine or more years this struggle was endured. One year the farm was abandoned and the family moved to town, where there were graded schools instead of the old district one-room school with twelve pupils. The town which had grown up in the neighborhood, that is to say some six or eight miles away, was Chadron. Finally Samuel Danley took his wife and the three granddaughters to Rocky Ford, Colorado. Here it was hoped there would also be cheap land and better agricultural conditions. But prosperity did not come. Grandpa Danley was by this time sixty-five years old, and he had lived a hard life. He died in Colorado in 1898, after the family had been there scarcely more than a year.

His wife returned to Chadron to stay with her son, William A. Danley, for the remaining six years which she lived. *The Chadron Journal,* Dawes County, Nebraska, of Friday, August 5, 1904, carried the following item:

> Mrs. Mary Danley died last Sunday morning at four o'clock at the home of her son in this city, after only seven hours of sickness, at the age of 65 years, 7 months and 17 days. The day before her demise she was apparently as well as ever, which accounted for the general surprise and shock felt all over the community when the news of her death became known.
>
> Mary Ellen Blair was born in McLean County, Illinois, December 14, 1838. In 1859 she married Rev. S. T. Danley, who preceded her to the world beyond about six years ago. They resided in the old home community until 1876 when they removed to Princeton, Ill. thence after three years to Niobrara, Nebraska, and two years later to Valentine, Nebraska, where they resided two years and then came on to what later became Chadron, where they remained until 1897. Their last move was to Colorado, where Mr. Danley died a year later.
>
> After his death Mrs. Danley came back to Chadron and made her home with her son W. A. Danley, where she has since resided. She was the mother of two children, a son and a daughter, the daughter, Mrs. John G. Stetter, having died about fourteen years ago in this city.

This left the three little sisters more or less at the mercy of fate. Their mother was dead and their father, although able-bodied and animated, was constantly "on the go" and at best was ill-fitted to be the caretaker of three such children.

PARENTS

John G. Stetter

John G. Stetter, the father of Leta Stetter, was born about 1855 in Virginia, and is still living at the time of this writing, 1943. His family are of German-speaking stock, and are said to have come to this country from the neighborhood of the Black Forest, settling first around Richmond, Virginia. There was apparently a large family but data are not available on the exact details.

He came to Nebraska as a boy of twenty, "driving a freight wagon." Two brothers, Henry and Jacob, also came either with him or at nearly the same time. They settled in the neighborhood of what is now Cherry County, Nebraska. The railroad was then being built through northern

Nebraska. The Rosebud Indian Agency was close by. At Fort Niobrara there was a military post. For all these enterprises considerable hauling and trucking of supplies, especially of meat, was needed. The brothers engaged in this work for a while, but in time they "took up land and went into the cattle business." Henry and Jacob long continued to engage in some phase of this business, as ranchers, feeders, traders, butchers, and dealers.

John G. was more restless than his brothers. He was also strongly gregarious, a good mimic, a lively dancer and banjo player. He was easily weaned from serious pursuits and became well known locally as a minstrel and entertainer of frontier type. He tried his hand at a great variety of enterprises, spasmodically and usually with some success at each, but always restlessly. He was a rancher, a peddler, a trader, a teamster, a cowboy, an absentee farmer, a speculator, and owned bars and entertainment halls.

Always garrulous and friendly, free with his resources to those for whom he had no responsibility, taking in fact all responsibility lightly, he became during his early and long residence on the frontier a well-known character in that corner of the state, and his name always provoked a tolerant smile of recognition. He was in fact always a boy, and never came to feel the burden of the world, as did his daughter, after him.

Physically he was short and heavy set. He was strong and quick, and light on his feet; he always wanted to dance a jig, and would do so, even in what should have been the most tragic moments of his aimless life. He was full of stories and exploits and inclined to round out each narrative with some sententious moral. For all his lack of schooling he had a certain native sagacity, and a marked verbal facility.

He was never amenable to the conventions of social intercourse and appeared, perhaps speciously, to take some pride in this negativism. He spoke with satisfaction of his early acquaintance with well-known frontier characters, such as Buffalo Bill, Old Jules, Jim Dahlman, and Sitting Bull. He declared that he had joined the Confederate Army as a drummer boy, although his birth in 1855 makes this improbable. Many of his tales were told for their interest value rather than for the sake of their authenticity. Of Johnny Stetter it could definitely be said that he was sociable, full of the joy of life, and sometimes generous.

In physique his eldest daughter Leta somewhat resembled him. She also was short, dark, and physically very strong. In a broomstick gripping contest she was more than a match for her husband. There was in her also a genuine zest for living, an insatiable curiosity, an inner protest against dogmas pronounced on flimsy bases, and an intolerance for bigotry, pomp and bluff. But in her there was no buffoonery and no clowning. Instead, her life was full of high purpose, a passion for beauty, and an eagerness to put order into the universe. If these latter traits were in her as a heritage, they came from the maternal side—from the Danleys, the Blairs and the McClures, rather than from the Black Forest.

Margaret Elinor Danley

Margaret Elinor Danley, the mother of Leta Stetter Hollingworth, was born near the old Danley homestead, near Danvers (formerly Stout's Grove), Illinois, on April 1, 1862, "on the Roop farm...one mile from Grandfather Blair's home."

She moved with her parents and brother to one farm or another near Danvers, then to Missouri, back to Danvers, and then to Princeton, Illinois. Here she attended a high school or academy, which subsequently developed into some kind of a minor college. The name of this institution at that time probably was Lincoln Academy. Since the Danley family left Illinois for Nebraska in 1879, this period of school attendance must have terminated in the seventeenth year of Margaret Elinor Danley's life. Further formal schooling than this she never received.

It was five years later, when she was twenty-two, that the Danley family settled near what is now Chadron, Nebraska. The region was then a part of Sioux County, and the year was 1884. Within another year the territory was politically reorganized and this region became a part of the newly formed Dawes County. The first marriage celebrated in the new County of Dawes in July, 1885, was that of Margaret Elinor Danley, now twenty-three years old, and the rollicking young cowboy minstrel, John G. Stetter.

On the 25th day of the following May, 1886, Leta Stetter was born in the dugout of her grandfather, Samuel T. Danley, at Dakota Junction on White River, near the town of Chadron. In her "home-coming letter" written December 3, 1937, to the *Nebraska State Journal,* she relates that "the person who officiated at my birth was not a doctor, nor a merchant, nor a chief, but a lawyer, Mrs. Fannie O'Linn, of Chadron."

This Mrs. O'Linn, with her pioneering spirit and versatile talents, was for years a friend of the Danley family. She was the subject of many appreciative oral narrations in the reminiscences of Leta Stetter in her maturity. For she herself became a vigorous advocate of the right of women to shape their own lives and follow their individual interests, free from the conventional restraints and taboos of the traditional domestic pattern. In Mrs. O'Linn she felt that she had early known a woman of just the independent character that she admired. There is indeed a singular appropriateness in the fact that Leta Stetter, in later years an active member of Heterodoxy, a club of able and achieving free professional women in New York City, should have been ushered into life by the hand of a woman who must in her day and way also have been something of a rebel.

After the birth of this first daughter in 1886, two other girls, Ruth Elinor and Margaret Carley, followed in quick succession. The three sisters were in fact born little more than a year apart.

But the mother, after giving birth to her last child, died the following day, February 9, 1890, leaving in the care of the rollicking young cowboy minstrel three infant daughters, all under four years of age. It was at this critical time that stalwart Grandpa and Grandma Danley, who had just managed to achieve a soddy or perhaps the log cabin in place of the original dugout, opened this shelter and the remaining years of their lives to the three orphan children, and cared for them for the next ten years or so.

Data concerning the appearance and personality of Margaret Elinor Danley Stetter are few. Her oldest daughter had of course no memories of her. There is however a photograph, saved and restored by this daughter, in whose personal letters to her biographer are also to be found a few characterizations, based on the remarks of people who remembered her mother. Such statements as the following are representative of the trend of these accounts.

> It is wonderful how she has "lived again" in the hearts of people. Gray-haired men and women peer at one through spectacles and say, "If you're half as good as your mother you'll be alright."
>
> After eighteen years one sees tears in the eyes of people who speak of her. Everybody knew her and everybody has memories of her.
>
> "Do you remember your mother, dear? She was a choice character, as rare as fine, frail china."
>
> Finally he talked about my mother. When I looked I saw that his eyes were full of tears. "She was the sweetest woman I ever knew," he said. "What a pity you girls never knew her."

(Another man) who was with her when she died looked solemnly at me. —Said he after a silence, "You'll never be as good as your mother, girl. Oh, you might be almost, but not quite. I tell you, I know what I'm talking about."

She was so small that her ring will not span my littlest finger, and she was too meek and tender-hearted for this world.

In this room is a linen "splasher" which she gave to my aunt when the latter was married. It is embroidered with the finest and most perfect stitches, with a design of vines and flying birds.

Downstairs, packed away in a box, are her botany specimens, exquisitely arranged and perfectly ordered. With them are her Latin books, and some finely written exercises, and a few books from the poets. Everything from her Latin sentences to the button-holes on her dresses has a kind of refinement in it.

Yesterday Mr. ——, a fat and jolly merchant after whom I used to name my dolls, took us riding in the country to where the old farm is. We went by way of the cemetery where that gentle and winsome lady, my mother, lies buried.

My aunt has a dish which she keeps carefully wrapped in tissue paper. "Don't you use this?" I asked her yesterday. "Oh, my, no!" she said. "Your mamma gave me that."

It is clear that Margaret Elinor Danley, whose father was a minister as well as a farmer, whose mother was well known as a gentle and gracious woman, and who had received not only the usual elementary schooling but had for some years also attended a high school or academy, possessed a richer set of accomplishments than did many of the women who came to the frontier.

To one who knew her oldest daughter it seems easy enough to discern traits and characteristics derived from the father and also traits derived from the mother. But such endeavors are probably wholly fanciful and the science of heredity is yet too little advanced for one to be sure of such judgments. Nevertheless it is tempting to say that one sees in the personality of Leta Stetter Hollingworth not only the stamina and animation of her minstrel father, but also the gentleness and appeal, and the quality of yearning, that seem to have been among the traits of her mother. But the caliber of her mind was peculiarly and uniquely hers, and there is nothing in her ancestry to have led one to expect it.

3

Birth and Infancy

The only record of the birth and infancy of Leta Stetter is to be found in twenty-four pages, written by her mother in a neat and clear hand, in a small red leather-bound notebook. This little book is still well preserved and the writing not at all faded. The book still bears on the inside of the front cover the cost mark, in pencil, RY/1.00. This was an amount of money not to be lightly spent in those days at Dakota Junction, and this well-bound, gold-edged book, which is empty except for the first twenty-four pages, well shows the taste and serious purposes of Margaret Elinor Danley Stetter in keeping the record of her child's development. The account is written in the first person, thus purporting to be the infant's own story of events. This record is here reproduced.

> I was born May 25th, 1886, Tuesday morning 12:30. Grandma and Mrs. Brainard dressed me then Mrs. O'Linn took me to the bed that my mamma was lying on for her to see me. She took me in her arms, kissed me, and said, "A little girl; isn't she sweet?"
>
> As soon as I saw Mamma I knew I would like her and we would have a nice time together. She was so glad that I was a girl instead of a boy. Grandpa and Dr. Davidson were there too and they all said I was a fine baby. They tied me up in Grandma's cook-apron and Grandpa weighed me and they said I weighed 8¼ pounds.
>
> I heard every word that was said but would not say one word myself. I could only look around and see and think I heard Mamma tell Grandpa to send a telegram to my Papa to come and see his little baby girl.
>
> Tuesday night Aunt Fanny O'Linn and Bessie came and stayed all night with me and I slept with Bessie all night.
>
> Wednesday Uncle Willie came home—was real glad to see me and thought I was a very pretty little niece. I know by the way he looked at me.
>
> In the afternoon Mamma and I were lying on the bed and I happened

to think of something funny and was smiling about it when Mamma saw me and called to Grandma to come quick and see me laugh. They seemed very much surprised to think I could smile. All the neighbors came to see me and make my acquaintance, I had callers almost every day for a while.

Now it was Friday and I had not seen my Papa yet. I was beginning to think I had no Papa or he was not very anxious to see his little girl. Uncle Willie sent him another telegram (Your daughter is crying for her pa!).

Aunt Fanny came every morning for a week and washed and dressed me and to see how I like to live in this world.

Wednesday morning I heard Grandma tell Mamma that she saw somebody walking up the road with a white hat on. Mamma said, "Maybe it is Johnnie." Then I heard the door open—a man came in, walked up to the bed, kissed Mamma, then took me up in his arms, sat down on a chair by the side of the bed and took a good look at me—laughed—and said, "It's the prettiest baby I ever saw."

I was looking at him too—I had been waiting eight days to see him and now I was wondering how well we would like each other. I had just about made up my mind that I was going to love him a great deal, when he said, "I'd give a thousand dollars if it was a boy."

That made me so mad but I could not talk and tell Papa what I thought of him just then. It made Mamma angry too I think, because she said, "I would not give her for half a dozen boys."

Mamma and Papa had a great time talking about and planning what they were going to do with me. Mamma had to show Papa my "footsy-pootsys," the dimples in my knees and elbows and my sweet little fat back.

The next morning when Grandma was washing and dressing me Papa had to come in and see how cute I looked in my little knit shirt. He said I looked like a little Dutchman sure enough then.

Mamma could scarcely decide what to name me. I remember she said she could not find a name sweet and pretty enough for me. I was wondering all the time why I did not have a name. Grandpa, Grandma and Uncle Willie and Papa said for Mamma to name me so she finally decided to name me Leta Anna,—Leta for a little cousin of Mamma's and Anna for Papa's sister. I did not like Papa very well yet because he had said he wished I had been a boy.

The first place I went visiting was to Aunt Fanny O'Linn's and Bessie's house when I was only a month old.

Mamma was almost afraid to take me to town "Fourth of July" for fear it would make me sick. But she wanted to go to see the Indians dance so she decided to go and take me. We went to Mrs. Carly's and I stayed there all the time. They thought I was too little to enjoy seeing the races, Indian dance, etc. In a short time after we got home that evening I took the colic. Grandma, Grandpa and Mamma walked the floor to make me hush crying but I had such a terrible pain in my stomach so I just had to cry and the tears rolled down my cheeks.

Mamma was scared because I cried so hard. Grandma gave me some little pills and put me into a bowl of warm water and I was soon well again. After that when I was sick or had a pain I wanted Grandma to take me be-

Birth and Infancy 17

cause I knew she could cure me. I thought then that I would never want to go to the "Fourth of July" again.

When I was about 7 weeks old one evening Grandpa was playing "boo" with me and I laughed out loud three times. Grandpa would say "boo, boo, boo" and then put his head down on my breast and it tickled me so I could not help but laugh.

Papa came to see me again in July. He sang to me and rocked me to sleep but I was not old enough to play very much with him. It would scare Grandpa and Grandma so when I would sit on Papa's hand and he would hold me out at arm's length. He sent me a nice cab so when it was nice weather I would ride in it outdoors.

One afternoon a few days before I was three months old I was sitting on Mamma's lap and she was rocking and singing "Juanita" to me. I watched her mouth and thought to myself "I believe I could sing too if I would only try" so I opened my mouth and commenced to sing as loud as I could. Grandma and Grandpa came and listened to me and they just laughed and laughed. After that I sang whenever I felt like it. Uncle Willie came home in a few days after that and Mamma told him I could sing. I was sitting on Grandma's lap and she said, "Now, Leta, sing your little song for Uncle Willie." She commenced "Juanita" and I sang just as loud as I could.

One morning soon after that I had just finished taking my "ninnie" and I put my face down under Mamma's and she said, "Where is Leta?" I looked up and laughed and then she said "Peek-a-boo." We played that then until we were both tired and after that I had lots of fun playing "Peek-a-boo."

The last of August Papa came up again to see me and I think he liked me pretty well now even if I was a girl.

In September Mamma was sick so I had to take cow's milk out of a bottle for a week. One night I waked up and cried. Grandma thought I was hungry so she got out of bed, went to the cellar for milk, warmed it over the candle, put it in the bottle and tried to make me suck it, but I would not and Grandma scolded me because I would not take it after she had fixed it so nice.

In October Papa came up and Mamma and I went back to Valentine with him to see Uncle Henry, Aunt Mary and my little cousin Anna, Uncle Jake, Aunt Emilie and Uncle Will. I liked Uncle Jake because he played so much with me, fed me at the table and gave me money to put in my bank, and Uncle Henry because he played on his banjo and sang for me. Cousin Charlie, two weeks older than me died on the 27th of September, so I never saw him and it made me feel sad to sit in his buggy and lie in his cradle.

I think it was the 8th of October that Papa, Mamma and Aunt Emilie and I went to the photograph gallery to have my pictures taken. I sat twice with my dress on, once for small cards, then for cabinets, then Mamma and Aunt Emilie took off all my clothes but my square and shirt and made me sit up there right before that man and I was so ashamed I wouldn't even smile because I was nearly naked.

Ma and Aunt Melie tried every way to make me laugh. Papa was holding me from behind the chair and I was so afraid he would let me fall and I put one hand around behind me and grabbed hold of the shawl. The man blew a little whistle; I opened my mouth and looked up at him and he "took me" that way with my mouth wide open.

We stayed at Uncle Jake's a week and then went to Uncle Henry's and stayed another week then Mamma and I came home alone on the cars. I liked to ride on the cars—it seemed as if someone was rocking me all the time. I slept nearly all the way there and back too. Grandpa met us at Chadron and I certainly was glad to get home to Grandma and Grandpa again, because I knew if I should have the colic Grandma could cure me. I was uneasy all the time I was away for fear I would take the colic and I did not know what I was going to do without Grandma.

When I was four months old I could hold out my hands to anyone that I wanted to take me. When I was a little past five months old one day Uncle Willie was playing with me and then put me on the bed with pillows all around me, but I surprised them all because I sat right up alone and needed no pillows to prop me up after that.

I ate Thanksgiving dinner with Bessie O'Linn. She came over to play with me nearly every week. Stella and Charlie Brainard came to play with me too sometimes.

When I was 6 weeks old I weighed 12 pounds and when 3 months only 12½ pounds, because I had so many bad spells of colic I could not grow much. At 5 months I weighed 16 lbs. and 8 months 18 lbs.

Papa came again the first of December and the 5th they took me to church at Mrs. O'Linn's house and had me christened. Mr. Powell a Congregational minister baptized me. I had my nicest long white dress on and I know I looked real sweet, at least everyone said I did. I did not cry but it frightened me a little when Mr. P. put the water on my forehead. I stayed to hear the sermon too. Mamma played the organ so I sat on Aunt Fanny's lap all the time and I was real good and listened to Mr. Powell talk and helped sing the songs as well as I could and everybody laughed at me because I tried to sing.

Papa and I had lots of fun playing dog, peek-a-boo, etc.

The 20th of November Mamma put my first short dress on. It was a brown flannel dress. Mamma said she felt like her little baby was gone and she had a little girl instead when she took my long clothes off. It was just the day before Thanksgiving that I got my first pair of leather shoes—I thought they were real pretty and I tried to unbutton and take them off.

When I was 6 months old I could play my own accompaniment on the guitar when I sang.

Christmas day was so cold and stormy that we stayed at home all day by ourselves. Mamma forgot to hang up my stocking so Santa Claus could not leave me anything but I got some Christmas presents anyway.

The 3rd of February I blowed my tin rattle box whistle, that Charlie Brainard gave to me, for the first time.

The last week in January I was trying to learn to crawl on the floor (I crawled backwards) and I guess I took cold for I had influenza Dr. Davidson said and I was so very sick that Mamma sent a telegram to Valentine for Papa to come. He came out and I was better in a few days and able to play "dog" with him. When I was sick I liked Grandma better than anyone else, she could hold me better and put me to sleep when no one else could.

When I was 7 months old I could say "Mamma" and "Dada" and when I was hungry I would say "Ninnie, ninnie."

When 9 months old I said bye-bye and after that when anyone would put on a hat or bonnet I would say bye-bye and hold out my hands to go out doors with them.

When I was 10 months old I said "Papa" and they would say "Where is Grandma?" and I would point my finger to her and when they would ask where Grandpa was I would point my finger to him. Grandpa taught me that the old turkey said "gobble-gobble" and the little calf "baa, baa" and the old cow "e-aw" and the old rooster "cuckoo."

I dearly loved pictures and Grandpa was the only one that would show me all I wanted to see.

One day I saw Fanny under the table—I was sitting on the floor—so I thought I would go to her and I soon learned I could go forwards as well as backwards and then I could go all over the room and get what I wanted and a great many things that Grandma and Mamma did not want me to have too. I thought everything was good to eat so everything I found on the floor I put in my mouth to taste. Grandma or Mamma would run to me and poke their finger in my mouth to see what I had put in it.

One day I tried to swallow something and couldn't so I was gagging and nearly choked. Mamma grabbed me and what do you think she found in my mouth—a piece of match. Mamma called to Grandma and was so frightened for fear I would be poisoned. She poured two teaspoonfuls of sweet oil down me. After that I was a little more careful what I put in my mouth, because I did not want to take any more oil.

I have three dolls, Jennie, Rosie and Mollie. Mamma gave Jennie to me when I was 5 months old and we have had lots of fun playing together. Uncle Willie gave Rosie to me for Christmas and Grandma gave Mollie to me. Rosie has both arms and one leg broken off so she is quite a cripple and such a care to me. I have to wash, dress and feed them all every day, and then rock them to sleep and sing "bye-baby-bye."

I have to help Grandpa feed the little calves and Grandma feed the baby chickens and turkeys. About the first of May Papa took me my first horseback ride on Prince, Mamma's pony. I held the reins and said "ho-ho" and "cluck-cluck."

The middle of May I went with Grandpa, Grandma and Mamma to town. Grandpa carried me into several stores and I had a nice time looking at the pretty things. I heard one woman on the street say "Oh, what a pretty baby," and another "What lovely eyes that baby has." One man gave me two oranges and a stick of candy but Mamma would not let me have them for fear I would get my dress dirty.

This is my birthday, the 25th of May. Just one year old today so I'll finish writing about a few of the events and happenings that I remember of the first year of my life.

I received some very nice birthday presents—an eating bib with a little girl and two little chickens and an old hen on it—from Charlie Brainard; a high chair from Mamma; a pink dress from Stella Brainard; a silver cup from Bessie and Hugh O'Linn, a doll from Grandma, a pretty little gold ring from Aunt Sarah, a nice gold necklace from Aunt Anna, and three gold dress buttons from cousin Baby Blair.

Just think—I am a whole year old. I'm not a little baby now but quite a big girl and weigh 19 pounds. I have two teeth and two others almost through and I feel very proud of them. I have been a real good girl during the whole year I think. Mamma scolds me sometimes when I am naughty but I just laugh at her because I know she wouldn't *dare* to whip me where Grandma and Grandpa are.

This somewhat fanciful story of the first year of her oldest daughter's life has a double value. In the first place it tells more about the character of the mother than has been gleaned from any other single source. Not only is there in it the gentle and affectionate feeling of mother for child; there is also a certain blithe lightness and gaiety, an easy imagination, and an intuitive appreciation of the probable feelings of her infant. There is a surprisingly apt attention to details of behavior and accomplishment, and a relation of them to the chronology of development that would do credit to a modern mother trained in the methods of child study. Little indications of developmental pace and progress in growth are recorded, such as have in the half-century since been seized upon by students of child development and standardized as significant signs of maturation and learning in the young.

The very existence of the account, written in this neat and accurate hand, in a sod or log cabin, or perhaps in the original dugout where the child was born, over fifty years ago, in the sandhills along the White River in Dawes County, Nebraska, tells much about the quality of this mother. So also does the simple fact that after several years spent in this dugout herself she could step into a congregation assembled at Mrs. O'Linn's and play the organ for the church service.

The usually absentee father, who appears tardily even when telegraphed for; who deplores the sex of his first-born and frightens the family by his brusque methods of handling the child; who, when he finally does show up, can be recognized far down the road by his white hat; who, before the infant is a year old, has her mounted on the back of a bronco, is also an instructive part of the picture, with resonances of many kinds in later years.

But the mother's perspicacious observations serve also to give the account a second value, one of which it is very unlikely that she ever dreamed. Many of the items reported in her more or less unguided record can be compared with the norms or indices of development now standardized on an age basis by students of mental growth. The earlier or later appearance of such items in the child's repertoire of behavior and maturation are presumed to be signs of the rate of development that has, up to the time of observation, characterized the child, and perhaps to point forward not only to the later pace of growth but also to the final level of attainment to be achieved. There are only a few of the items here noted that have been thus standardized, but there are enough to give strong evidence of the quality of the organism of Leta Stetter.

An interesting list of items, the date when they made their appearance in this particular infant as compared to the age level of a child of normal rate of growth, can be constructed from this amazing mother's record.

Item	Average Age of Appearance	Appearance in This Instance
First smile	5 weeks	2nd day
Laughter	8 to 16 weeks	7 weeks
Visually directed reaching	18 weeks	16 weeks
Sitting up unaided	33 weeks	21 weeks
Begins to imitate	4th month	Before 3 months
Creeps	10th month	8 months
Says "Papa" and "Mamma"	14th month	7 months

Progress in weight lags somewhat behind the average schedule, and there is nothing precocious in the dates of appearance of the teeth. These more or less structural traits show no more than average development pace. But the more functional characteristics, showing themselves in the infant's behavior and activity, give a different picture. Seven of the items reported have found a place in the "normal schedules of development," although there is considerable variation in their dates of exhibition by different infants.

In all seven of these indicators the first daughter of Margaret Elinor Danley Stetter ran far ahead of expectation. She smiled, laughed, reached, sat up alone, began to imitate others, crept, and began to make use of language a good deal earlier than the average child can do these things. And the more symbolic these items, as in the use of language, the greater the discrepancy between this child and the average expectation. This is precisely the picture we have now learned to be that of the gifted individual. During her first year of development Leta Stetter was, so far as signs of intelligence are concerned, far "ahead of her time." She continued to show this characteristic throughout life, and her achievements, whatever she undertook, were always far beyond those that anyone had any good reason to expect from a human being selected at random.

Years later Leta Stetter found this little book, bound in red leather, and in a personal letter wrote the following paragraph about it:

> In it my mother wrote down everything I thought and did during the first year of my life. Her idea was to write down all my thoughts till I was old enough to set them down for myself.
>
> With what ease and simplicity she was able to "become as a little child" in order to do this. And I find that I was much wiser in those days than I am now or perhaps ever shall be.
>
> If I ever again attain to the simplicity and dignity of that first year, I shall be glad, for I thought no evil of any person.

4

Childhood

Records relating to the first twelve years of childhood are meager indeed, except for the period of the first year so carefully reported by the mother. Leta Stetter's earliest memories, as she once recorded in print, were of "Texas long-horns, Sioux Indians, blizzards, sod houses, our log house, and the one-room log schoolhouse where I attended from six to ten years of age." In a letter she described this little log schoolhouse, "where as a child I dug powder-post out of the worm-eaten logs and administered the same, when the teacher was elsewhere engaged, to the pupils seated near me as medicine."

But she also remembered well enough the farm, her grandfather's homestead, and many of the activities there. "The farm is there also, where at the tender age of eight I learned to milk cows." There she helped her grandfather plant and husk corn, and feed the horses and cattle; and likewise she helped her grandmother with the chickens and turkeys. It was here also that she acquired a life-long phobia for cows, after a long-horned animal attacked and nearly gored her before it was driven off.

> Do you love to reassume the consciousness of childhood, and feel yourself running your fingers through the oats in the horses' box, or recall the odor of pumpkin, freshly chopped up for the cows?
>
> November, 1906

There were memories of the interior of this log cabin, and of some of the characteristics and activities of the grandparents, as shown in the following:

> Their house (a farm family) reminds me so much of my grandparents': old-fashioned pictures in oval frames on the wall, a "motto" worked in yarn, a family album and a family Bible on the center table, and watermelon pickles and doughnuts on the table in the living room.
>
> November, 1906
>
> Three years ago grandmother died.—Poor, poor grandmother! her life had not been an easy one. It had been that of a Nebraska pioneer woman and she had come from a refined and sheltered home in the eastern states. But she bore it bravely and died unembittered by any hardship.
>
> She had a little trunk up in the room that was hers. In it were all the family trinkets she had saved for years. Silver spoons given as prizes at county fairs, silk patch-work things that had belonged to our mother. She had written little notes to us girls, probably in the wistful months when we had never (been allowed) to answer her letters, and had pinned them to these articles.—Some of these things we took home with us.
>
> January 25, 1907

There are further memories of the grandmother, which introduce also the picture of another adult, vindictive, to say the least, who had later assumed responsibility for the supervision of the three little sisters.

> When we girls first came "home" to live she took a most violent dislike to the grandmother with whom we had been living, because of certain things the latter had said, presumably. But *really*, I think, because our grandmother belonged to the family of our mother. She refused to have our grandmother in the house and we children (aged nine, eleven and thirteen respectively) being plunged into this new and unaccustomed association were in mortal terror almost of our lives and took to fleeing when our grandmother came near because we knew what would happen if we were to do what we wished.
>
> Poor old lady! My grandmother was as good and as peaceful an old lady as ever blessed the earth. She went to Chadron to live with her son there. And often she would spend her slender allowance to come to V— to see us girls. At such times she stayed at my uncle's house, and I still remember how she would stand at their gate, shading her eyes with her hand, to see us girls on our way to school. And we, miserable little cowards—it certainly seems to me that we were even then old enough to be called cowards for such

an action—would "pass by on the other side" for fear ——— would find out that we had gone across.

Poor, sweet-natured old lady! After eight years the sight of her standing there mutely at Uncle's gate wrings my soul with the keenest regret I know.

January 25, 1907

Some of the outstanding memories of these early years on the homestead had to do with the worries of the grandparents over poverty, debt, grasshoppers and drouth. There was also a remembered concern over the welfare of the two younger sisters—a concern that continued to the last days of Leta Stetter's life. There were little memories of play activities, of accidents, of gifts and special clothing, and of such chores as children of that age could undertake. But the outstanding memories were of "moments of beauty," and an esthetic sensitivity that characterized her throughout her life was manifested as far back as memory went.

She used to sit and hold a Bible "just because I liked to feel the paper in it. My grandmother thought one was fast coming to the Lord, but it was only the paper manufacturer one was worshipping." She remembered going out into the field where the dry, hard stalks of corn stood in winter "to watch the sunsets through the corn."

> If I looked from the dooryard there was the whole richly glowing sky of the west before me; but I would have none of it. I loved it so much better through the standing stalks of corn.
> November, 1906

Sunsets, especially those of fall and winter, always held her interest, and her letters often refer to them, and sometimes deftly describe them.

> And when there is a gray wall of cloud down the horizon, with just a single crack of dull red rimming the boundary of the earth, I nearly always watch it till it is gone.
> November, 1906

Even as a little child her esthetic responses were strong and conscious.

> Before I was seven I still recall the sobs that used to overcome me when the sweetness of birds' singing or the silence of evening laid their message on my inarticulate, childish soul. . . . The pain of my own experience is yet very clear to me. It was pain because

there was no means or outlet for its expression, for it gripped me too young . . . before I knew the medium of sentences or of written words that can make a sunset burn or a flower bloom forever."

January, 1907

Before she was ten years old, while still living in the log cabin on that isolated homestead on White River, she had made a compact with life, formulating a life plan, and "renounced the rest of childhood," as she sat one day in an old weather-beaten sleigh. And life, she averred, went on in the pathway where she then set it.

It seems uncanny to me now, noting many children, that when I was less than ten years old I had taken a look at life and decided that in order to be "competitive" some period of it must be left out. . . . I had read in some book that man's life is divided into stages and this put the uncanny idea of omitting one of them into my head. I should be frightened if any ten year old child should say such things to me now, but then I never opened my mouth on the subject, so nobody but you knows or ever knew of that solemnly kept compact with life—that if I left out part of childhood I should be granted other values which seemed more to be desired. . . . I decided to grow up then and there, solemnly renouncing the rest of childhood. . . . Nor has life failed thus far to keep the compact.

July, 1906

Thus the infant, who during her first year was in intellectual respects "ahead of her time," continued to speed her developmental pace. How restless that juvenile mind must have been for activities for which the barren surroundings of the sandhills provided no material. Even the school activities were trivial and unexciting to one who had renounced the rest of childhood. Her chief interests, aside from enjoying the beauty of natural events around her, came thus to be verbal. She was from her earliest years supremely interested in words, in phrases, and began to make verses and compositions of her own even before she could have become acquainted with many of those made by other people.

I used to ponder over things found in Readers. Never shall I forget
> *There is a story I have heard,*
> *A poet learned it from a bird.*

And the "Burning of Moscow" flames forth as vividly on my mind as it did then. . . . Perhaps the reason I cried because I couldn't "read numbers in the thousands" was because I looked so steadfastly on such things.

May, 1907

There remains from her early school days a tiny memorandum book packed full of quotations, maxims, and proverbs, written in a round, childish hand, and gleaned from one can scarcely imagine what variety of sources. Her uncle, Wm. A. Danley, in a letter to her of date March 16, 1924, says:

> I have been intending to write and thank you for THAT BOOK. It certainly is interesting, and I remember so well when you was about three feet tall out on White River how you used to talk about writing a BOOK.

All these interests persisted and ripened, and ultimately became essential parts of life for Leta Stetter. In view of them, one can easily see why it was that after finishing high school she went on to the university, became Reader in English literature, was elected Class Poet of her college class, and wrote ceaselessly thereafter. Although little is revealed of her life during these first ten years, that little, interestingly enough, was what became the very core of her later personality.

The years from twelve to sixteen she spent with her sisters at "home" in Valentine, with her father, who in earlier years had been the rollicking cowboy minstrel. He was now engaged in slightly more sedate pursuits, and he had again married. There was from the beginning uncongeniality between children and stepmother, and the father was poorly equipped to act as mediator. Memories of these years are full of misery, and the scars there received by a sensitive child persisted no one knows how long into her later life. Not only the home situation but the general conditions of life and standards of behavior in that primitive frontier town fitted poorly into the spirit of the beauty-loving child, just torn from the beneficent care of her pious and gentle grandparents.

A brief epitome of the "home" picture, leaving out some of the more distressing features, is to be found in the following characterization:

> Now, apropos of the situation at "home"—there is certainly enough material there for an eight-volume novel; a five-act melodrama; a treatise on "The Psychology of the Quarrel"; an essay on "Step Children: How to Thwart Their Evil Designs"; a sonnet on "That Impudent Child"; a short story entitled "I Want Twenty Dollars"; a popular song called "I Don't Want to Go to Chicago"; a . . . but the resource is simply inexhaustible. Hollinshead and Sir

Thomas Mallory's "Hystorie of England" aren't a circumstance, when it comes to material for literature.

November 8, 1908

A full account of conditions under which the growing girls spent their four or more years under these circumstances would involve detailed descriptions of individuals who are only by the mercy of God and the laws of man entitled to get into this picture at all. For the most part they may be spared.

The more amiable features of the paternal personality may be seen in the following description:

> He certainly is one of the kindest men that ever lived. . . . In some ways he never grew up. As he himself expresses it "a Dutchman never develops mentally till he's forty-five." He *never* dresses up. I've *never* seen him wearing what he calls "a paper colar and a claw-hammer coat." On the two or three occasions of his appearance in church—once when old A. was buried, once when little Sis "spoke a piece" at the Christmas tree, and once at revival meetin' when One-Armed T. "spoke," he wore a suit of clothes *much* the worse for wear, an old felt hat that had seen many better days, and his big dog-skin overcoat.
>
> May 20, 1908

For the girls, these were strenuous, as well as disagreeable years, but in the process they acquired domestic training and skills which they never outgrew. Housework became for them a matter of course, to be tossed off lightly in the free hours left from school attendance.

> For the first year of our being at "home" she had a servant girl to do the work, and . . . when this girl left because she was unable to get along with her, we girls worked every minute we were not in school, getting up every morning at five o'clock and doing everything we could before school time, doing the heavy sweeping on Saturdays, and the baking on Sundays. The washing and ironing was practically the only piece of work that was left for someone else, and a washwoman attended to that.
>
> January 7, 1908

Something of the general conditions of life in a far western town during these formative years may be gleaned from a letter describing, not the town of Valentine, to be sure, but another place in which Leta Stetter was visiting at the time:

> On the whole one may say briefly that it is a typical far western town. The spirit of the "early days" still survives. One sees the "slickery" tin-horn gambler pass by on the street, flashing a sparkler big as a doorknob, and the cowboy in his red shirt shouts thro' the town on his broncho.
> There is much to be observed. Broadway simply isn't in it for powder and paint. The cases in the drug stores are full of these "staples" and the practical application thereof is something to marvel at.
> The town is full of soldiers who jolly with these pink and white beauties, and of army officers who pass them proudly by on their dancing horses. In truth these horses are the finest, most intelligent creatures one finds in (town)—the cavalry horses, you know. Their slender bodies shine like satin from the grooming, and their well-turned hoofs and legs perform gracefully when the band plays. They are thoroughbreds, from hoofs to restless ears, and I love to look at them.
> July 3, 1908

There are also a few descriptions of the "home" town; it must of course be borne in mind that with the development of modern transportation all western towns have become pretty much alike. But in the old days each town had its own unique flavor.

> The Indians have come down from the reservation, and are making night hideous with their dancing. Yesterday Mr. Poor Dog, a tall bony Indian with a smile that wouldn't come off, stepped up to the back door, and with signs that would have done credit to Doc in Race Psychology, demanded a bass drum. We assured him that he had "called up the wrong number," and he went away still smiling.
> July 15, 1906

> There are some not uninteresting people here, too, if one stops to take account of them. Mrs. Z., who "finished a musical education" in Paris and is now a farmer, also has a buffalo coat given to her by her first husband. Mr. S. who "has twice saved his life by ducking lightning"; Arkansas Zang who once nearly rode a buckskin pony to death looking for it all over the prairie....
> July 18, 1907

The characters and episodes around her she early began to observe as material for possible "stories," and in her college years some of these stories materialized.

> Now said stories sound rather flat and a little pale to one who was born (romantically) in a "dugout" on White River bottom in 1886, has cooked custard pie for "Arkansas Bob" and "Mose," and who has lived on the plains of the Mole-Eye Kid who "had the makin's of a man if he hadn't throwed in with Long-Shorty and Peg-leg Magee."
> Mr. B. should have heard some of "Arkansas Bob's" inimitable yarns, told in his own original "style" before starting out on his literary career as a "portrayer" of the West. Some day when I get time I'm going to "ante" with one of "Arkansas's" yarns, "raise Mr. B. back," "deal" to some publisher and "stay." Like enough I'll have to "lay down my hand" finally, but there's no harm done in running a bluff, even if it is called by the other fellow.
> August 31, 1907

Favorite among her diversions in these childhood days in Valentine, when there was time for diversion to be spared from the "fiery furnace," was horseback riding. Among her fondest memories were those of horses she had then known. So long as she lived she retained a lively interest in horses. She knew most of the records of the leading horses at the races, certainly those of the conspicuous champions. She attended, in maturity, the horse races in the East at least once, but was disappointed in what she found there. But the Horse Show in New York was one of her favorite spectacles, and she attended it repeatedly. Another quotation shows this interest in horses:

> The horseback ride of Wednesday night was great. There was a party of fifteen, and the moon was big and bright. My horse was Jim, and he and I went on ahead and had the hard road to ourselves for rods at a time. It was dandy! Jim is the best saddler in the barn; he never trots, he is thoroughly bridle-wise, he has no fool tricks, and won't let anything under saddle pass him, once he's in the spirit of the ride. So we just galloped on and on for about fourteen miles.
> November 6, 1908

5

High-School Days

The conditions for scholastic achievement, under the circumstances just outlined, must have been anything but favorable. But high-school graduation was achieved with good standing, and encouragement was given by the teachers that had much to do with Leta Stetter's future. The general conditions and their unpropitious character are briefly suggested in the following excerpts:

> They ought not to have expected mere children to bear their burdens, yet many and many a night I have gone to bed, and so have my sisters, wearily wondering what a day would bring forth in the way of strife and turmoil. . . . You cannot realize, for syllables will ever halt in their effort to convey life. . . .
> You have never lain awake all night, when you were thirteen and fifteen to see in what condition . . . nor stood calmly day after day and heard yourself accused. . . .
> And you have not (or at least I pray that you have not) then gone to school daily with your brain in a turmoil from these experiences and worked like the very Dickens for your soul's salvation.
> October, 1908

In the Class of 1902 at Valentine there were six girls and two boys. The smallest girl was Leta Stetter, who, when the diplomas were signed, May 23, by H. W. Koenig, Moderator, and J. C. Pettijohn, Secretary, was still fifteen years old. She would however be sixteen on the day after tomorrow, May 25th.

Her high-school records have not been examined, but the transcript provided by the University of Nebraska reports her as admitted, "Conditions O.K.," from Valentine High School (3 yrs. '02) with the following credits toward entrance requirements of 30 points.

Algebra	3	History	3
Botany	1	Latin	7
English	4	Physiography	1
Geometry Pl.	2	Physics	1
Geometry Sol.	1	Civics	1
German	2	Physiology	1
General	1		

The high-school principal at Valentine at this time was Robert H. Watson, subsequently candidate on the Democratic ticket for the office of State Superintendent of Instruction. He was clearly an effective and inspiring school man, to those capable of inspiration. Leta Stetter rated him highly, and she was herself an educator of experience when this rating was reported:

> That good, good man, my old high-school superintendent (must be thanked) if anything of the truly spiritual has been permitted to live in me. . . . remembering my own great need and the good man who by the spirit in his face kept alive for me faith in high things.
> April, 1907
>
> I tried to tell my old teacher what he had done for me, and that that influence would go on as far as I went, if that were a short way or a long way. I thought I was far enough away from the past so I could bear to speak of it, but before I knew it life had flowed tremendously back from those high, white walls, and choked utterance.
> August, 1906

In spite of the hardships of her early life, Leta Stetter never regretted that her place of origin had been on the western frontier. She maintained a loyal enthusiasm for her native state throughout her career, although it does not follow that she ever approved of the local conditions under which she was reared and lived through her adolescence.

> I shall never cease to rejoice that I was born on the limitless prairies. To grow up on their expanse means to "see in long stretches," to scorn boundaries, to go "free" all one's life. Down around Fremont one sees carefully tilled "eighty acre farms," and sleepy do-

mesticated animals. But two hundred miles west begin the rolling plains; and how one's heart leaps up to behold them!

June, 1907

The environmental difficulties which scarred the souls of the three little sisters had nothing to do with domestic duties nor with study. They issued instead from the clash of psychopathic personalities and from the irresponsibility and coarseness that were perhaps more common on the western border than among the steadier and more successful individuals who had remained behind in the East. Paranoid personalities, domineering and vengeful, might hope for easier adaptation in a sparser population. Dipsomania was a common addiction and was sometimes only a defense reaction against other and more deeply seated forms of imbalance. Certain forms of roughness might even have appeared for the time to have a survival value, and profligate indifference in the distribution of one's resources was easily given, on selfish grounds, a sort of social sanction by other irresponsibles. It was easy enough for a combination of eccentricities to generate an atmosphere and a regime that to little children could seem like nothing but "a fiery furnace."

Against the bitter circumstances of their lives the eldest child, from ten to sixteen, struggled first to reform the clinical conditions, then at least to defend the peace. She finally set about steps to snap the bonds that kept the situation tense and cruel.

> I pray that you may never know anything like the tortures that scorch the "fountain of tears" dry before one is sixteen. . . . Only those who have passed through can tell you what you have escaped.
>
> September, 1906
>
> Well, anyway it makes dreadful unhappiness and nervousness and worrying. After awhile one gets where one simply can't see clearly. "There's no place like home"—thank God.
>
> December, 1907
>
> One should undoubtedly always deal gently with the temperamentally diseased, but one also owes a duty to the young and normal and growing, a duty that *must* be performed, at whatever cost of doubt and self-questioning and worry. That duty I performed. . . . I will never undo it.
>
> January, 1908
>
> How horribly the memory of all those bitter and terrible days . . . recurred to me. With what real agony the past scenes cramp one's

nerves! . . . Sometimes when I sit quite alone and busy, suddenly the terror from which I have forever fled comes back to me, not *really*, of course, but none the less clearly, especially if something has reminded me of it. . . . I suppose terror can become as much a habit as anything else.

August, 1908

Now I wash my hands of all their affairs forever. And thank the good Lord I am quit *forever* of that dreadful place. I feel that it would choke me ever to set foot upon its "threshold" again; so terribly do I remember it.

October, 1908

It will be observed in these accounts that the real escape from the "fiery furnace" was not accomplished until the oldest daughter had torn herself away, put herself mainly on her own resources through college, and was in a position, if need be, to act with power and insight. These fragmentary hints of the "fiery furnace" are revealed here only for the sake of calling attention to some of their possible later consequences.

In the subsequent development of Leta Stetter, the problems of human adjustment, and the difficulties of the young, combined with a professional interest in the mentally deficient and diseased, became conspicuous, and many of her own distinguished contributions were in these fields. It is permitted to a biographer to seek to find in earlier years the seeds of more mature interests and the motivations of adult activities. It is above doubt that here we are on the trail of such influences.

Among the influences that clearly contributed toward the character and aspiration of Leta Stetter must be reckoned not only heredity, her teachers, and her childhood experience, but also the picture of her almost unremembered mother's traits.

Yesterday when I was standing by the place where she has lain for eighteen years, you don't know what an agony seized my throat. I thought of all her gentleness, of all her fineness, of all her winsomeness, and of her suffering. . . . And if she were alive now, how would I not strive to recompense and reward her as much as in me lay.

But I have a fancy, as I have had since I came to know what manner of woman she was, that one may do that even though she died so long ago that I cannot remember her face. . . . If at any time I do true or worthy things it is and will be because my mother's spirit has had power "to live again in minds made better." . . .

I think of her always as one whom I might have in some way shielded if she had lived, might have cared for and protected. . . .

Nobody knows how I have longed for her to be alive. It sounds queer, doesn't it, but there is no "mere emotion" about it. It is a definite pain that goes to my throat and has hurt me ever since I "grew up." Do you ever wonder about your mother, too, and love her after all these years? For I think . . . that you will understand just what I mean.

July, 1907

The earliest record available of anything written by Leta Stetter is a poem of seven verses, written at about the age of fourteen, while she was in high school. The poem celebrates the Lone Pine, which stood on a high elevation near the town of Valentine, Nebraska. This eminence, with its solitary tree, was a familiar landmark in the vicinity, and the poem was at that time printed by the local Valentine newspaper. It is here reproduced.

LONE PINE

High up, on the peak of the hill-top,
  Where the tempests meet in strife,
Thro' the night and the storm and the darkness
  It stands like a lonesome life.

Beaten and scarred and crippled,
  By the winds and rain made old,
While the pine trees down in the valley
  Are sheltered from storm and cold.

From a barren rock on the summit
  Of the hill it lifts its form,
Alike to the warm spring sunshine
  And the fury of the storm.

Silent and uncomplaining,
  Except when the sad winds moan
Thro' its broken and battered branches,
  The tale of a life, alone.

High up where the world may see it,
  Sharp outlined against the sky,
While its brothers down in the valley
  Unnoticed are all passed by.

And the Lone Pine standing patient,
  Where the wild winds wage their strife,
Beaten and scarred and crippled,
  Like a broken, lonely life,

Is telling again the story,
  As the winds thro' its branches moan,
Of a soul lifted high o'er its brothers
  That must bear the storm alone.

Subsequent to the death of its author, this poem was printed for private circulation in a small collection of her verse, and was read by Professor Lewis M. Terman, well known for his life-long studies of the gifted. He writes, of his own accord:

> I am glad you included the poem written in her early teens. That is comparable to the very best poetry written around that age by any of my one thousand gifted children.

Among the verses found in her papers there was the beginning of a collection which was apparently to have been called "Prairie Years." Many of these had not yet been written, or at least no copies of them have been found. Some were recorded and there was a list of titles of intended verses, the topics of which all refer to these early days in northwestern Nebraska. These titles are:

The Corn	Prairie Dog Town
Prairie Years	White River
Old Times	Wild Currants
The Autumn Necklace	Homestead
The Movers	The Soddy

Others of the poems in this collection have a youthful touch, and may possibly have been written in high-school years, although most of those in the privately printed collection were written in freshman and sophomore years in college. Those which may possibly have been written this early, and those which refer in subject matter to the objects and experiences of these early years are reproduced at this point also. They are, "The Round Window," "Papoose," and "When I Was a Little Child."

There are other verses, some tentatively outlined, some represented by a few initial lines. Only those have been used that appear to have been completed to the author's satisfaction. There is, however, no indication that she felt them to be worthy of publication. Some of them may have been class exercises. Some of them took the place of letters in personal correspondence.

THE ROUND WINDOW

Once when I was a little child
I played by the old gray sea,
And a tower to sunset turning
With a great round window burning,
Like a red eye, looked at me.

Like a round, red, bloodshot eye!
I was only a child, you see,—
And it looked so wicked glaring,
And it looked so angry staring,
That it hurt the heart of me.

PAPOOSE

Close your eyes, dear little child.
Hear! The coyotes call afar
Where the Day Chief's tepees are,
And the west wind breathes so mild
Through the gold beams of the star.

Pale-face women showed to me
As I sat here yesterday
The picture of a child away
Underneath a star, and he
Is a God-child, so they say.

Close your eyes, dear little child.
Little dark child with dark hair.
The God-child's face was spirit fair
Like the white man's,—but he smiled
Like the little babe I bare.

WHEN I WAS A LITTLE CHILD

When I was a child I can remember how
The fairies came and taught me all their plays,
And led me forth into the golden ways
Where they went, and they told me magic words,
And made me understand the songs of birds,—
    I have forgotten now.

And how the sweet-faced women gently smiled
And held me in their arms and every one
Was good and happy. When the day was done
My mother kept me safely on her knee
And softly sang a little prayer for me,—
    When I was a child.

6

College Years

Upon graduation from high school in 1902 Leta Stetter was enabled by her family to enter the University of Nebraska as a freshman. There is no record of the precise reason for her having gone to this institution rather than to one of the several smaller denominational colleges in the state, or to one of the State Normal Schools, as did her sisters for a time, later. The choice was probably guided in part by the advice of teachers, but it is reasonably certain that Leta Stetter's own discernment had a voice also in the matter.

For this year, at least, suitable provision was made for the life of a student in the state capital, and the living allowance was sufficient to maintain her in a comfortable room with a private family. Although this provision was not continued in later years, for the time being it enabled the sixteen-year-old to give her whole attention, during the critical first year, to her studies and to enter actively into the social life of the campus.

She once recorded an impression associated with her first arrival at Lincoln to enter the University:

> I shall never forget a certain "immediate" moment which touched the consciousness as the train took me into Lincoln for the first time. The journey . . . had made me dead tired, and I laid my head down on the window-sill and felt the grind and movement of the whole thundering train. An "emotion" of the irresistible swept over me, an "impression" of inevitable movement and destination, if you will. (That is poorly expressed but I dare say it will tell you). And the thought flashed through me that my life must always be like that, and the thought bound itself up with the visual memory of a red sun setting across farms. Then at last we alighted from the train and saw for the first time the buildings of the old

University to the east. But I have always remembered the strange "immediacy" of that moment.

June 11, 1907

During the Freshman year she was enrolled for English, German, French, English Literature and Physical Education, in both half-years. Four hours of the German credit is recorded as having counted back on entrance points. Her grades this year, for the academic subjects were 27 hours E (Excellent) and 10 hours G (Good).

In the Sophomore year her studies included English (two full-year courses), English Literature (two full-year courses), German, French, Geology, Philosophy (Psychology), and Physical Education. Grades for the academic subjects were 29 hours E, 2 hours G, and 2 hours (Graduate Seminar) P.

The program for her Junior year included Education, Rhetoric, Philosophy (Psychology), German, English Literature, European History. The grades were E for everything except a G+ in a 2-hour Psychology course.

Her subjects in Senior year were English Literature, Botany, Geology, Philosophy (Psychology), Greek, Latin, European History, and Education. The grades this year were almost evenly divided between E (18 hours) and G (19 hours).

The relative slump in academic standing in the Senior year had many and diverse causes. She was entirely on her own financially, or practically so, and spent many hours weekly as a departmental assistant. She was involved in extra-curricular affairs, such as sorority and fraternity life, class committees, publications, and organizations. Social affairs claimed her constantly. There were severe worries connected with the "fiery furnace," from which she was not by any means free. Most handicapping perhaps of all, at the beginning of the year she became engaged to a classmate, and spent many fond hours wandering with him away from academic responsibilities. Finally, she had postponed to this last year the laboratory sciences in which her interest, and perhaps her aptitude, was weaker than in the literary fields which occupied her program almost exclusively in the first three years.

This four-year college record was of outstanding quality, and in literature and creative writing she achieved a campus reputation.* One of

---

*She was literary editor of *The Daily Nebraskan*; associate editor of *The Sombrero*, "the Undergraduate Book of the University," 1906; and assistant editor of *The Senior Book*, Class of 1906.

her instructors, while she was yet a Sophomore, persuaded her to send some of her writing to several of the high-class magazines, but she did not yet find entrance there. She was admitted to advanced seminars in her field, by special consent. She was an active and contributing member of the English Club. Beginning with her Sophomore year she was appointed Reader in the department of English Literature, and carried this responsibility along with her own studies, for the remainder of her time at the University.

During her Freshman year she joined the Chi Omega sorority, and later was elected a member of other campus groups. Upon graduation in May, 1906, with the B.A. degree, she was awarded election to the honorary fraternity of Phi Beta Kappa, on the basis of her scholarship. She was designated Class Poet by the Class of 1906. The Class Poem, which was read and printed in connection with the Commencement ceremonies, is here reproduced.

ALWAYS AND FOREVER ROSES DIE

One thinks when some dear, gladsome time is done,
"What if thro' all the rounds and rounds of years,
The heart should lose it!" and the sudden tears
Spring hurting to the eyes. Well, this is one
Of all those times of which an end must be;
How shall its life be kept for you and me?

Oh, never weep with him of bitter heart
I once saw pausing where white roses die
And hide the earth in fragrance where they lie.
With darkened eyes he looked, then turned apart,
And murmuring hopeless to himself, he said,
"The thorns still sharpen when the flowers are dead."

Another came and stood within the place
Where softly breathing lay the living snow,
And looked upon the waste and bending low,
Stooped as he loved it. Then I saw his face!
He gathered all the petals at his feet
And thro' his life they gave him fragrance sweet.

So we may know what wisdom is, we read
Its mighty meaning in the brow and eyes
Of him who knows to keep his paradise
In fragrance when the living thing is dead.

> *He looked so calm, for tho' his eyes were wet*
> *His face was placid and without regret.*
>
> *This story runs in sweet and tender ways,*
> *For always and forever roses die*
> *And all about us fragrant petals lie;*
> *The remnants of the precious, perfect days*
> *Which come and pass. But mem'ry still may lend*
> *A fragrance sweet to gladden to the end.*

The writer, who was the classmate already referred to, first saw Leta Stetter when he went to the University of Nebraska as a Sophomore in 1903–04. Her personality and appearance attracted attention. She was small, lithe and graceful, with a lively gait and a characteristic lilt to her gestures. And she was full of enthusiasm and animation, unpretending and friendly.

She used to frequent a remote stack room in the library, where the heavier volumes on anthropology, philosophy, psychology, and social science were shelved. Usually this room, if peopled at all, contained worried adult graduate students working on theses and a few unduly sober majors in philosophy and psychology. I first observed her on her frequent visits to these somber quarters, wearing a bright scarlet Tam-O-Shanter on her dark hair, and poring over one or another of the giant tomes. She brought a new and brighter note into the dusty stack room.

From this point on our acquaintance ripened and endured* until, left behind after a third of a century of comradeship, I am trying, on these pages, to tell the story of her life and work. But the details of that association may be told elsewhere, and that part of her story will not appear in this volume.

Leta Stetter showed, from the beginning of her college course, a dominant interest in literature and in creative writing, particularly when it dealt with human relations. During her Freshman and Sophomore years, in addition to the prose themes and assignments, she tried her hand at writing poetry, again and again. No diligence was exercised in preserving these things, for they were most modestly regarded by her. In fact, when such of them as it has been possible to collect were finally

---

*We were bracketed in the *Senior Year Book* as members of The University Bluffers Club.

run to ground, they were not found among her own papers, but in the hands of others who treasured them.

In the privately printed collection of her verse, distributed after her death to a few of her closer friends and associates, twenty-two poems were included. Five of these have already been given on these pages. Of those remaining, seven are pretty definitely known to have been written in later years, subsequent to her marriage. This leaves perhaps ten in the collection "Prairie Years" that were written in college. All of these, according to her own statement, were written in her Freshman and Sophomore Years, when she was sixteen and seventeen years old. These poems represent as best they can the trend of her recorded subjective interests during middle adolescence. They are here reproduced.

A PHILOSOPHER

Gray are these walls of Oxford and they wear
That dimness that old tho'ts and musings cast
Over a city, reared in the long past
For heark'ning to God's Word, and for the care
Of that strange dream, that mystically, somewhere,
God's voice must speak to comfort man, at last.
Now from the cloisters quick, new murmurs fast
Break forth,—no echo of a dull word-prayer
Nor of a lip-worn ritual wearisome.
Now all the altars are left void and lone.
From list'ning for God's voice that still is dumb,
Thro' all the ages silent as the stone,
Man turns his soul, and sees young science come,
Free, open eyed, to claim all for her own.

JOHN THE BAPTIST

And he said, "I am the voice of one
Crying in the wilderness." No Rabbi he;
He was but born to preach his blessed Lord,
Jesus, the Saviour, and asked no reward
Except the knowledge of his duty done
And that the people all might turn and see
The heavenly kingdom waiting there at hand,
And follow Jesus in his ministry.
He must decrease; the people must forget

The humble hermit when the Saviour came;
All this he knew, and meekly did accept
His fate, and in his stern, strong heart he kept
The lamp of loyalty forever set
Burning and burning like a holy flame.
Yet in his wanderings thro' Judah's land,
Bearing the tidings in the Christ's pure name.
No woman ministered unto his need,
Sternness and strength ungraced by any touch
Of lovely things,—this was his way of life;
No hearth was his; no home, no child, no wife,
Nothing of these, for these are but for such
As bear no burden of great word and deed.
And so he said "I am the voice,
The voice in the wilderness, crying that all may hear."

THE HERMIT

I am a hermit. Let the sad world roll
On with its burdens and its pain and strife.
I look to a better and a higher life,
For I shall chasten and preserve my soul.
From all the world's wild cares I make me free,
And naught have I to do with human pain,
Nor have I fear of loss nor greed of gain,—
And yet I heard them say they pitied me.

A WIDOW

Make not your glance so brief!
Do you not understand?
This dim blue gown, with cornflowers down
The breast, and its yellow band,
Instead of the gown of grief?
Make not your glance so brief!
Can you not understand?
Oh, he loved dim blue, and the cornflower's hue!
He would love this gown with its band
Instead of the gown of grief.

THE LISTENER

The song of great, harmonious winds that blow
Around a canyon at the close of day
Made yearning in the world. And far away
The sundown, like a sacrifice burnt low,
Flared red and flamed. Old, solitary, slow,
The hour passed, brooding, staring on its way,
A prophet among hours,—as on whom lay
The burden and necessity to know
And cry God's word. There quick my listening mind
Harked to old dreams, and trembling—eager caught
A sudden faith up. Here perhaps to find
The Burning Bush!
But listening, I heard naught
For God has never spoken since mankind
Let go fair, flashing fancy and seized thought.

AN OLD WIFE

When my man died they slipped to me
And telled me he war gone, but I
Said nary word, nor did not cry.
Nor did not fall. It seemed t'be
As if war some queer, sad lie.

An' even when I hearn the sod
Drop in the grave, I did not beg
Him back, nor moan like John and Meg.
But afterwards . . . at home . . . Oh, God!
Thar war his old coat . . . on its peg!

An' I've prayed long to God, but he
This time can't hear nor answer me.

TWILIGHT

Twilight creeping over the world;
The noises of night in the quiet land;
Wavelets lapping the level sand,
Where the shore and the water meet and part;
Twilight lying calm on the heart
Like a brooding dove, with its soft wings furled.

CRYING IN THE WILDERNESS

Out in God's wilderness the creepers run
And mind their own wild will. The untaught trees
Stand glorious in earthly pride. The sun
At setting throws its long thin jets of light
Like a crimson fountain on the wayward world.
And seldom man has broke that silence, for
The finger of awe lies heavy on his lips
    When he steps there.

But this thought leaps up in me like a joy:
If any man should raise his voice out there—
Out in the waiting wilderness should cry
Aloud with faith a thundering prophecy—
How long and grandly down that infinite
A crying voice might tremble all the leaves,
    And echo and thrill—

THE MARCH FROM FAUST

Let not your faith be abated!
Onward! onward! marching along.
Men, have courage and be strong!
What if the petty rage and fret,
What if the weakling hearts forget?
Stand by life with a calm repose,
Have faith in the task,—God surely knows
Why his world was created.

RUSKIN

"Blessed are the pure in heart for they shall see
God,"—it is the promise of the Christ
Made on the mount . . . Ruskin, that spirit-man,
Who knew the truth about what life could mean,
And rose up calmly to reposeful deeds
Of self-renunciation, and lived on
Still meek and pure in heart,—he saw his God
In human faces and in flow'rs and thoughts,
And gave to us the vision that he saw.

7

Life Plans

At the time of completing her college course Leta Stetter's real wish was for some kind of a career connected with literature—with books and their writing. For one thing, she believed that the short story, only lately come into vogue, was to develop into one of the most expressive mediums of communication.

> I got a book of short stories last night by Bruno Lessing. They are sketches from the life of the New York Ghetto, brought together under the title *The Children of Men*. Some of them are well done, with grace and "suggestiveness," but they lack "form." They are not "crystal clear." I tell you . . . there is not one writer of short stories that can equal or has equalled those old French fellows,—Balzac, Maupassant, Daudet. We have no rival for them in our own language, the German has none (German minds do not work "deftly" as do the French). The Scandinavian offers them no competitor, so far as I know (which is not very far . . .) and even the Italians do not equal them.
>
> "I hold" that the short story is to be the literary form of the coming "age." Everything tends that way. Concentration of thought and energy, the growing evolution (observe the tautology) toward greater brevity, the busy life of the people. The time has come when the eight-volume novel of the past is condensed and abbreviated to the Short Story. Even the one-volume novel is beginning to see the prospects of its future, and to gather, with its companions in one and two volumes on the shelf.
>
> So I am always looking at the books of men and women who write in this literary form, for the masters of our day will be writers of short stories, and I look for the Master, but cannot find him yet. There is always something "unmasterful" to be found. . . .

But those old Frenchmen,—there is the sweetest charm in them, and at the same time the most lurid fancy, and the strangest imagination. Emotion played on them as the winds on the strings of some delicate instrument and the result is so nearly like music that one can linger and linger after the logical sequence of words. They can create a story from just an emotion, and make it hurt the heart, or touch it with charm and gladness.

November 2, 1906

Remarks in the same vein may be quoted from her comments on another book she had been reading:

(She) has insight, even though she writes pages and pages before she gets to it. (She) cannot write "short stories," more's the pity, . . . those endless pages discourage one, so one turns aside . . . before one has even touched its problem. . . . The demand for "condensed" moments of joy and vision, . . . the short story.

May 20, 1907

Moreover, she wanted to depart from the usual theme of the literature she found currently about her:

Why should *every* popular novel of these days have for its theme, or at least for one of its themes, the pursuit and satisfaction of illicit love? Why do they all seem bent to "proceed upon the theory that the Seventh Commandment is the only commandment and that the principal attraction of life lies in the opportunity of breaking it,"—as Van Dyke said of French matinee plays? Surely the great thing we call Life is infinitely broader and greater than that one theme.

What would become of the passions of worship, mercy, self-sacrifice, honor, love of wisdom, truth, courage, and the thousand others, if we had only the "popular novel" to read and believe and mould our world by? Of course, one must believe, who has experienced it, that true love is the most uplifting and glorifying of all the passions; but it is not the *only* passion, and there is as much inspiration and strength and joy in "The March from Faust" as there is in the Bedouin Love Song.

August 16, 1908

She had tried her hand at writing stories, and continued to do so in rare moments of leisure, in later years. There is in fact a collection of seven stories by her, only one of which has appeared in print.

The presence of this ambition to write is no novel trait of the bright adolescent. But Leta Stetter had no undue opinion of her literary gift. The urge in her was a deep but an unassuming one. Meantime, it was necessary to earn a living. She was resolved no longer to commit herself to the scenes of her distressed childhood, and there were the sore needs of others, whom she was determined to save because of her profound affection for them.

> Sometimes I read that meaningful myth about the three who were cast into the fiery furnace and how they came forth unscathed because of great faith in high things. . . . But there is always a dreadful danger of perishing. And so I could care a great deal for . . . and for . . . I suppose Meshak cared a great deal for Shadrak and Abednego after they finally emerged from the flames; don't you suppose so?
>
> August, 1906

This subordination of her own aims and wishes to the needs of others, felt by her to be in some way worthy, was steadily characteristic of Leta Stetter, always. In her very last months and years she was devoting her resources, her time, and her energy, to the salvaging of less valuable personalities, while many of her own creative projects were longer and longer postponed.

Evidences of the strong urge to express herself in writing are frequent in letters written during the year of her graduation from college, and in the year or two thereafter. Toward this aim, moreover, her college teachers had confidently urged her.

> Do you really think that I could "write"? Somehow I always feel the quotation marks around that word. There is an incipiency in the term which grows out of associating it with the inefficient,—aspiring youths, ungrammatical maidens, local "poets," and English Club members; all those who feel spasmodic up-wellings of emotion, and imagine that there is a reason why these experiences should be chronicled on paper.
>
> But what things are required of one who will really "write"? The power to see far and farther, general knowledge, acquaintance with all that has gone before, mechanical means (perfect mastery of his language), the power to put his thoughts uniquely and artistically, and the power to make people love him. He must catch the vision of his own age, furthermore, and must produce that for which there is demand. And if he have all these requisites and his work

be not in some way unique and peculiarly helpful and serviceful, it is a failure.

The problem of "demand" for written work need trouble one but little. If a thing is worthy it will find its place. . . . If one's efforts find no place in the "scheme of things," let him rest calm in the assurance that they were in some way wanting.

I am possessed of a kind of curiosity to discover where (my own) "boundaries" are placed. . . . Someday perhaps I shall tell the old world what it looks like to me,—after I get through taking a look. Then, perhaps I never shall. Perhaps when I have acquired all those things which I have yet to learn, I shall feel that my service could not be worth while, or more probably the class of people known as editors or publishers will feel so. Yet almost always I feel that it would be the most exhilarating fun in the world to "write."

October, 1906

"What is literature, primarily?" he asked. And I said that primarily and essentially it is *theme*,—theme in evolution, if we view it through the ages.

He slapped his knee and laughed. "They will not accept it!" he said. "There isn't a man of them who will take it. They are all death on the history, or the 'form,' or the mechanics, or the 'influence' of one man on another, or the development of phrases."

Then he asked me if I thought I could hold fast to my idea, wherever I went and whomsoever I heard. For he said it was hard to keep such a belief among the "wise men of the East."

And hesitatingly he also said that my province lay not among the critical but among the creative; that he always had hoped and always would hope for me such a place.

. . . that same old "promise" looming up on the horizon again. And whether it will ever be fulfilled, the Lord only knows.

June 18, 1907

She was constantly haunted by the spontaneous arousal and perseveration of phrases, verbal patterns, and ready-made sentences. These she enjoyed lingering over and wondering about. It seemed to her that they cried for development and were the keys to themes such as she might rejoice in unfolding.

This has been the "funniest" day with me. Do you ever get "spells" when you are simply unable to pursue the work which the moment demands, and when your mind persists in concerning itself with the most impertinent and "inopportune" subjects? Well, this has been such a day with me.

"Things" have been insistently "occurring" to me, all day long,— whole sentences, ready-made, float into my mind in the midst of the conjugation of the German verb. For instance:

"A noise dropped into the silence and splashed there in widening circles of sound." or—

"Three men sat under lamplight, around an oblong table." or—

"A line of red rimmed the horizon."

Then I jerk my mind resolutely back to the future tense of the verb *loben,* only to find it wandering off again after some hereto unconceived figure, glimmering vaguely through the dark blue dusk of evening, moving indefinitely down a thread of road, with a bundle slung on a stick behind it, and peering eyes fixed somewhere "off beyond." . . .

For instance, this sentence came to me while I was sewing, all formed and ready-made:

"A coarse hand, dripping with dirty water, thrust a scrub-brush under the window, and scrubbed and scrubbed vigorously on the outer ledge."

That was all there was to it, but it persisted in my mind, and seemed to be always suggesting some sordidly realistic bit of life behind itself.

I presume you are laughing at me by this time, and it is *funny,* but it's so just the same. These "ideas," if you could so name them, are entirely impertinent to my daily labor. But really, they entertain me a lot, and it's interesting to examine them and "develop" them during assembly period when everybody is "being good."

November 23, 1908

And here is another account, in much the same vein, but written a few days later.

With regard to the ready-made sentences that come and go through my head, let me tell you some more of them:

1—"She went blandly about the rooms, distributing a few handshakes where she judged they would do the most good."

2—"When darkness fell he went disheartened back across the prairie, and did not know that he had 'wrung blood from a turnip.'"

3—"'This,' he said, looking with spiritless eyes, 'is the Burden of the Desert.'"

> 4—"The man looked down the slant of hillside, and in the green hollow sheep and lambs were grazing, peaceful in the sunshine; and he felt through all his troubled being the simple influence of primitive things, and of Life as it was in the beginning."
>
> etc. etc. ad infinitum.
>
> Now you can readily see that there is no logical connection between or among these sentences. Some of them are not very "good"; some are suggestive; some contain peculiar word combinations. They interest me greatly.
>
> As for "testing" them sometime by unfolding the suggestive ones into "themes," I certainly shall do that some day. Perhaps I could not keep from doing it, but as for the popular "success" of these same "developments," I have my doubts. . . .
>
> One must make a theme "marketable" before one can spring it on the unsuspecting public. Nes pa? Hence it occurs that the "profession of literature" is extremely uncertain and few (comparatively) there be that find it.
>
> However, all this to the contrary notwithstanding, let us have a crack at this business. . . . And if by any chance men should care about the little true and beautiful and brave and happy and pitiful things in human life that have hurt or healed *our* hearts, then let them take for their own souls' good the vision that has seemed "good" to us. If not, let them go whither they *can* find food.
>
> November 29, 1908

Her incidental memory, for things not deliberately regarded for the purpose of retention, was remarkable, all her life. She seemed never to forget anything that she had seen or heard, or that had happened to her.

> Sometimes I rejoice in my "desultory memory," and just little snatches of things pass through my mind,—texts, verses, visual memories of fine faces seen in crowds and portraits, little melodies with a "tune" in them, little "noble" acts of people one has known or heard about. . . . Sometimes I think of things I read, sometimes of people alive in this world, sometimes of the meanings and events of history. . . . And "texts,"—is it not curious to observe how all the abstract wisdom of human life as lived and conceived of, has concentrated and articulated itself in "texts"?

But this preoccupation with literary forms and themes had, for the time being, to give way to more practical considerations. Her solution, for the immediate future, was to prepare herself for the teaching of high-school subjects, preferably literature and language. In her college program she designedly included courses in Education which would, upon graduation, qualify her for a teacher's diploma.

Along with the diploma reciting her qualifications for the degree of Bachelor of Arts, dated June 14, 1906, she received a State Teacher's Certificate. This certificate recites that having "successfully completed, in addition to other studies, the requirements of the University Teachers Course, consisting of two years of special and professional study," the recipient is "qualified without further examination to teach in any of the public schools of the State of Nebraska." Furthermore, it is recorded that this recipient is "recommended as especially fitted to teach English Language and Literature."

There is also on this certificate a "summary of record" showing the distribution, by departments, of the work of the recipient while a university student. Arranged in order of decreasing magnitude these figures are:

Subject	Credits
English Literature	25
English Language	17
Germanic Languages	15
Romance Languages and Literature	14
Psychology	11
European History	10
Education	10
Botany	8
Greek History and Literature	6
Roman History and Literature	4
Zoology	3
Physical Education	3
Geology	2
Total	128

8

A High-School Teacher

A month before her commencement day, on May 16, 1906, Leta Stetter signed her first school contract—with School District No. 6, Saline County (the town of DeWitt) Nebraska—to serve as the assistant principal of the high school "in a faithful and efficient manner for the term of nine months." In return the Director and Moderator of said school district covenanted "to pay said Teacher the sum of $60 per month for said services, and to keep the schoolhouse in good repair, to provide the necessary fuel and supplies, and to furnish janitor work."

And so, "commencing on the 3rd day of September, 1906," in conformity with this contract, Leta Stetter began her first year as a high-school teacher, as it happened in the home town of the man she had promised to marry. His family still lived thereabouts, as they had done for three generations, and she had, during that year, ample opportunity to explore his background and reputation before committing herself irrevocably.

However, instead of English Language and Literature, which she had been certified as competent to teach, she was assigned English, Latin, German, History, Physiology, Civics, and Botany, for "seven forty-five minute periods per day."

The town of DeWitt was a village of less than 1,000 people, but children came to high school also from the adjoining farm school districts. The town was in the southeastern, agricultural corner of the state. There were eleven or twelve grades, the last three or four of which were taught by the principal and his assistant. Equipment was meager, and many of the pupils were poorly prepared and not scholastically eager. The new principal was the graduate of a State Normal School. Living conditions in the town were still simple and in some respects primitive.

Leta Stetter found living accommodations, after much inquiry, and such as they were, with an elderly widow who owned and occupied a house by herself, but had to find her meals elsewhere. The general conditions of life, the heavy and miscellaneous program, the backward pupils, and the seriousness with which the first year of teaching was undertaken, made this a strenuous and in many ways a disheartening experience. But her teaching was welcomed and in time appreciated and praised, and it was with expressed reluctance that the community saw her depart, at the end of the year, and with her contract richly fulfilled. She was to teach, for a better salary, not everything, but the subjects for which she had been prepared, English and German, in the new and progressive high school of McCook, in the southwestern part of the state.

A few excerpts from letters may serve to reveal her impressions of these two towns and exhibit the diversity of educational conditions existing in the state of Nebraska at that time. First a few comments about DeWitt, where she had been told by the principal that "you see, I always made a special study of grammar and there ain't much I ain't taught about it one time and another."

> Instead of the funny little room, made hideous with wild-eyed family portraits, behold the two spacious front rooms of Mrs. M. Instead of the 1 candle kerosene lamp which smoked its chimney daily, two excellent electric lights illuminate our "suite"; instead of the employment of various and sundry devices found necessary and apparently customary at B.'s one finds a good bath tub with plenty of hot water. . . . It used to be positively ironical the way Mrs. B. would insist on dealing out "wash rags" with nary a bath tub on the premises. But she never perceived the pathos of the situation, nor the need of such an article. To her mind the galvanized washtub was a good deal more than sufficient for all purposes.
>
> September 27, 1907
>
> Take it all together, it's as different from last year's first day as though it wasn't the same profession. Instead of Mr. X. walking in with a button off his vest, and the need of a shave, Mr. T. enters casually at the close of the session, with immaculate shirt-waist front and smooth-shaven visage and beams upon one, inquiring after the progress of the day.
>
> Instead of a handful of wretchedly prepared ninth graders, who never saw a note-book, I find fifty bright and shining freshmen to whom a note-book is as familiar as the shoes on their feet. Instead

of cracked and scarred black-boards I discover smooth slate surfaces. Instead of a hardly-to-be-played-on organ, a well tuned piano gives out the march, etc. etc. In short, history is *not* repeating itself.

September, 1907

Here one finds little rosy-cheeked ninth-grade boys who "will bring your mail up for you in the morning, Miss Stetter"; tall twelfth-grade fellows who open doors for one and stand graciously aside while one enters the class room; nice little eleventh-grade boys, who sit near one in the cafe in company with their mammas and have excellent table manners; tenth-grade girls who "would like to call on you soon, Miss Stetter"; twelfth-grade girls who approach one in the spirit of fellowship; and prim little freshman girls who look neither to the right nor to the left during school hours.

September 27, 1907

It was, nevertheless, not easy to leave the first town where the school board had trusted her and appointed her in spite of her lack of experience, and where they had loyally supported her work.

Thursday afternoon, and the lessons have all been said! One lone botany student wrestles with "specimens" in the recitation room. The corn, planted three months ago in a window-box, stands high and green against the light. The "Daily Program" that I placed on the board that first day, stares emptily back at me. It no longer means anything. Algebra problems in cube root straggle wearily down and across the front board, and on the left questions interrogative of the "Mexican War" confront one as one turns. Webster (unabridged) looks older than he did nine months ago, and the piles of text books stand on the front desks exactly as they did that first morning. They look like "history repeating itself." Chalk dust lies thick and white on the organ cover. . . .

Never more . . . shall I hear of "President Johnson's impeachment, and was it justified?" Never more of Napoleon's second war. Never more of the "lymphatics and the glossopharyngeal nerve." It is finished.

And after all, I am not all glad. It always has been and it always will be hard for me to face the crucial moment of "uprooting." One finds then to how many little unsuspected affections one has become subject. All the little "happy-go-luckies" and "didn't realizes" whom I had to fail came and said they wished they'd "have you for our teacher next year." I marvel more and more at the development of the sentiment of justice in youngsters.

And how the "decorating" of the "graduating class" carries one back to a time five years gone by, when one gave an oration redolent of "noble sentiments" and looked up at one's motto—ROWING, NOT DRIFTING, on the wall.

May 24, 1907

On a visit the next year to the little town of DeWitt her reaction was far from enthusiastic:

Well, this is just the same old place, almost "word for word." . . . but in general things "is as they was." I'm glad to see folks, but some way I have no desire to go near the school building. The everlasting weariness of the day, the unsatisfying routine that held me to that place still burdens me when I look at it. I can almost feel the chalk dust.

December 23, 1907

The newer town, as such, remained interesting and hopeful, although, before the second year there had transpired, an unruly school, confronting an unwelcome principal who had lost control, made teaching wearisome.

I have looked around at the town a little today and it is truly "quite a place." The streets are all laid out in blocks like a city, and the walks are all cement, some laid in mosaic patterns. The houses are dignified with street numbers and electric carriages roll about with quite the nonchalance of Greater New York. Moreover the youth disport themselves in patent oxfords with large bows, and in trousers pressed and distinctly "in fashion," and the high-school girls are quite as foxy as those of Lincoln High. There are four or five thousand inhabitants; a school which employs fine teachers; with a superintendent who is thoroughly efficient, well-known and up to date.

DeWitt was hopelessly static, finished, done with; McCook is young, vigorous, adolescent, growing, dynamic in every way. . . . In short, I like the place.

September 16, 1907

These accounts and quotations have been given here at some length, not because the characteristics of two communities have anything to do with the life of Leta Stetter, but only to show the nature of her reactions to life, the character of her comments on and about it, and the general tone of her letters. She taught in this second high school for the year 1907–08, and began a second year there, the year 1908–09. But by this time the long delayed marriage with her university classmate became possible. He had gone to New York City where he was working in Columbia University for his Ph.D. in psychology, and was assistant in the department there.

By the middle of the academic year 1908–09 it became economically possible for the two to join hands and pitch their tent together in the East. Leta Stetter therefore resigned her position in the McCook High School, and when new arrangements had been made for carrying on her work there, she paid her folks in Valentine a short visit, then went to New York City. She was married there, December 31, 1908, to Harry L. Hollingworth, and was associated with Columbia University for the remainder of her life.

9

Attitudes and Viewpoints

Leta Stetter by no means abandoned the field of education when she left the state of Nebraska; she was, on the contrary, engaged in this field all her life. Nor did she forget her early desire to write; she wrote prolifically for the rest of her days. The precise way in which this synthesis of activities was achieved will be the main theme of much of the remainder of this volume.

Before following her from her native state into the East, a group of further excerpts from letters written while still in Nebraska and quoted here will reveal at least a partial picture of the quality and variety of her interests. They suggest something of her attitude toward life in the earlier years of her maturity, and something of the élan with which she went forth to meet that life.

Her attitudes as a teacher are briefly indicated in the following fragments from some of her letters. They tell also, in part, why throughout her lifetime her students, young and old, developed such enthusiastic affection for her.

> Yesterday we dissected an eye and observed the crystaline lens, the choroid, the sclerotic coat, the retina, the cornea, the iris, the optic nerve, etc. Furthermore we saw a drop of blood under the microscope and dug into the convolutions of a brain. I have no doubt that Prof. P. would have had a fit of prostration if he could have heard the oral dissertation on structure and origin which I delivered to that wide-eyed and credulous "graduating class." They were that interested that they remained after school to "pursue the subject further."
>
> Last week also the history class received a lecture on the Survival of the Fittest, as exemplified in the "march of history." . . . We are

just finishing the Roman Empire. Next comes Medieval Europe, and Christianity.

The joyous gods have given place to the Christ. Sometimes . . . I have a kind of sadness to think that Great Pan is dead. He was such a light-hearted god! But when the race outgrew childhood it demanded something more than just joy; so Pan died.

January 12, 1907

Furthermore, the other day a Freshman girl came tiptoeing into my room and said abruptly, "I heard something. I heard you said we could see God in *people*, if we tried. Did you say that?"

I asked her to sit down and explained, as I had previously to an upper class, that every person has something "divine" in him if we are "pure in heart" enough to see it.

The child listened attentively to every word. When I finished, "I believe that too," she said. "They were talking about it, and I wanted to know." . . .

When I think of all these manifold "instances," my throat begins to hurt, and I fear lest some day in German class I shall burst out spontaneously into weeping and wailing.

December 2, 1908

But I have little daily psychologies of my own here in this "beautiful little city." This week it has been the boys who smoke, God bless them. I have a surprisingly large number in the Freshman class. I am taking them one by one and "talking" to them. Today it was little X., round-eyed and brown. When he passed my desk with note-books I said, "I want to see you, X." So he sat very still in his seat when the others were gone, and waited the approach.

"X., you smoke," I said. His face flushed. "Yes'm," he admitted, looking at me straight.

"Do you think I tell the truth when I say that's the reason you're poor in your work?"

"Yes'm, I know you do."

"Well X. (I love him for his name) can you tell me just why you smoke?"

He was silent a full minute, willing, even eager to tell, but unable to articulate it. "Aw, I can't tell, you just have to, an' you do."

"Is it like being hungry?"

"Yes'm, only worse."

Then I said, noting the coming tears, "Do you think I think you're a bad boy, X., because you smoke?"

The poor little youngster bit his lip, and gazed hard upon the floor. He is about fourteen.

I assured him gently, gently, that I did not think him bad. And then the full confidence of the heart of a boy came to meet me.

"I wish't a thousand times I never learnt, but I can't promise you I'll quit, 'cause I'll do it again, an' the other boys, they won't stop; so I can't, an' it's gittin' worse all the time, even the little fellers git it, an' once I was sick for two months and couldn't, and then I never thought about it till I got where the other fellers had it, an' I started in again, an' Dutch, I know he won't quit an' we're good chums."

"Now," I said. "Don't you promise me you'll quit. Don't promise anything you can't do. But don't you know that if you could stand the struggle for three months it would go away, and it would be over?"

"Yes'm," he said, "it would, but I'd go to smash in school work while it was lastin'."

Poor little feller! pesky little sinner! It hurt me to keep from putting my arm tight around him and placing my cheek by his.

We talked some more, and at last he said, "I might slow down, but you don't *know* how it is that I can't jest quit sudden, like tomorrow."

"Yes, I do, X.; yes, I do," I said, and when he went it was agreed that he was to "slow down."

Bless these loyal little hearts! It is a trouble to them, when finally one finds the real boy behind his "self-defence," and when they once get started they will tell you "all they can." But it is pathetic how it grips and spoils them.

November 8, 1907

The next group of paragraphs, chosen almost at random from many expressions of this character to be found in her letters, show glimpses of her general viewpoint on several common topics, at about the age of twenty years.

Yesterday I went to church with G. . . . The preacher is distinctly denunciatory in his attitude toward the world and all that dwell therein. He sees no naturalness in anything, so obsessed is he with "doctrine." He grows so excited in his contemplation of Science and its evils that he forgets the Scriptural quotation which he is about to give and slams the bible under his fist so that the noise vibrates. When I see him striding before his audience, and recognize in him the type of a wide-spread class, I feel a peculiar satisfaction in remembering that God was not in the earthquake, nor in the fire, but only at last in "the still small voice."

October 1, 1906

... the men and women who have written, they cannot get away from their own personality. They feel the types and meanings of their own individual spirits, and take these to be the types and meanings of the Universe. They "paint" the thing as they see it, and earnestly insist that it is the thing, *as it is*. Perhaps no human being will ever be able to throw off this limitation of "personality" and be able to behold the Universe uncolored and unchanged by his own types.

Do you know any mind in the past that has been strong and fine enough to do it? I cannot think of any. Some have come very close to this supreme vision. Christ stood high in its pure light, so did Plato, and to me (perhaps not to you) Ruskin did. But yet all of these men lent to the light the hue of his own "personal equation." They saw the same Truth, but each "applied" it a little differently. Their conclusions are not identical. . . . Will it ever be possible for any man to step forth from the influences of his own types, and interpret the Universe *as it is?*

September 20, 1906

It is one of my most indispensable theories, that the soul is the ultimate substance, the body merely the mechanics of the combination. And I believe it to be a true idea for, so far as I can observe, those who have lived by the opposite hypothesis have not led "happy" lives, hence must have found themselves out of harmony with the great "system" which punishes only untrue things. . . . There is no "illusion" in holding the soul above the body, so long as the body be recognized and properly cared for "as such."

February 22, 1907

When people break The Law, as it is writ large on the world for all, I *want* them to suffer. I have a perfect passion for wishing to see them "pay." If they seem not to suffer retribution I feel somehow cheated. I cannot "from my heart" *forgive* them and wish to see them escape consequences. Oh, it is easy enough to speak with them as usual, to regard them without malice, to treat them conventionally. But I do not absolve them; I can't forgive them till they've paid.

Now you see . . . I don't mean at all my "enemies," that is those who may dislike me, or harm me, or differ from me in values or opinions. Bless you, no! I can absolve them easily enough; or rather, I can't, for there's nothing to forgive them for. But those who "offend against God's holy Law," for instance against the law of kindness, or of meekness, or of generosity. I just delight in seeing them suffer the penalty.

August 18, 1907

Sometimes I almost shake with the joy of thinking that I live in *this* day of the world, and that before I die I shall see the coming of a new religion, which is to touch the hearts of all the hungering people through Science and Scientists.

November 18, 1908

Nearly all of the wisest and tenderest of them ("texts") were said by our friend J. Christ. Surely his "everlasting life" with its loving kindness is one of the most transcendent instances of the power and dignity of "spirit" and the far-reaching strength of a "dreamer of dreams." I like to picture to myself the ways he went in the world, how he walked among the people in his seamless robe and blessed the children, how he chose the publican to be his friend and follower, how he forgave the woman who had sinned, and cast out devils and spoke gently to Judas and to Peter. I wonder at his infinite vision regarding the sins and mistakes of mankind, and his pity; at his great capacity for quietness in the presence of crises. . . . He had several faults, but he believed in "spirit," and just for that he has influenced the events of history and "saved" individuals years after his body was dead.

July 26, 1908

And how truly has this belief in "things not seen" served me all my days! For, my God! supposing I had believed only in things seen, where would I be now? Supposing I had accepted only the *facts* of the existence and the environment where I was obliged to grow up! What would have become of me?

But I perceived, someway, the intangible essence of "spirit" in the world, and I followed it away from the *facts* by which I was surrounded, and how true that "spirit" has always been to me. . . .

If "spirit" is a "man-made, mental substitute" . . . I can only say that it's about the best job "man" ever did, and that "man" deserves a lot of credit for inventing same.

September, 1908

As for me . . . quite possibly I shall not fulfill the "promise" of my adolescence. Some kind of "promise" I conclude there was or is to the external world, for I never had but one instructor who did not bring it verbally to my notice. It grew into a kind of little game, to see how long it would take them to say it.

April, 1907

A teacher said to me at the end of one school year a long time ago, that he hoped I would live a long time, for if I lived long enough I could do certain things. And I remember that I stood off from his remark and looked at it, for I was old enough then to look at things critically.

October, 1906

The next few quotations from some of her letters disclose the character of her literary values in her youth, and express some of her critical comments on things read at that time.

> Are there any people writing now in the English language whose thoughts and words you could care to see live and live? So far as I know, and my knowledge is very limited, there are just two people writing books (fiction, I mean) whose influence I could care to see go on and on. One is James Lane Allen; the other is James M. Barrie.
> Of course there are many faults to be found (by Dr. Sherman) with these men's work, and they are probably not Great Masters, not Dantes nor Goethes nor Shakespeares. But their thoughts and sayings have in them the most exquisite appreciation, the purest fragrance, the most touching melody, the sweetest meditation and the clearest vision, and I love to read and read them, drawing the life out of them.

November 22, 1906

> But it is a fancy of mine that all creative souls die with some "necessary" vision unuttered in their hearts and that they wait wistfully, watching those who have yet the privilege of life, to see whether some one will not utter it. Of course . . . they die with many things unsaid. It is unthinkable that Carlyle or Emerson or Elizabeth Browning had said all they could before they died; they were obliged to leave much unexpressed; and then, likely there were things that they never could have expressed at all, because they were not the proper "mediums." There are seers yet to come.

May 9, 1907

> As heretofore threatened, I have been reading Mallory. Of course he is hopelessly verbose when read by one in the twentieth century, but the archaic diction tastes good and the charm of "fair ladyes" lies gracious on his pages. One thinks with that old English writer, whose name I no longer remember, "Live ever, sweete booke"; but it has already "lived ever" without the aid of one's thinking.

September 8, 1907

> Do you know, there *was* a "chair of literature" under whom I could have cared greatly to "work." I never could have done so, for this "chair" was in a college which repudiates the "fair sex" (per-

haps being so dark, they might have admitted me), and now the "chair" is held by some one else. The man to whom I refer is Henry VanDyke, formerly of Princeton. To me Brander and Professor Trent and Carpenter and all the rest are as "dry bones" in comparison. All that I ever read of his is full of the beauty and the tenderness of "theme," rich with the imaginings of a loving spirit, and alight with the discernment of a "seeing eye" and an "understanding heart." He has no mania for "mechanism"; neither is he an analysisomaniac, nor has he any "fixed ideas" on the subject of the history of language, neither regarding verbs or adverbs.

Have you ever read his "Ruling Passion?" I found it in the library and read it the other night. You may remember that I once said to you, "Why do people write always about 'love,' so called? Why can't they write about will, and ambition, and honor and long suffering, and a thousand other things as strong and exalting as love is?"

Well, VanDyke, it seems, also thought that very thought, and then he set out to make a book illustrative of the truth of the idea. It is a volume of short stories, and in them he shows forth those "other passions, no less real, which also have their place and power in human life—music, children, nature, honor, strife, revenge, money, pride, friendship, loyalty, duty...."

And the pages are gently wrought by this man who lived "the gentle life." It was he who prayed, "Help me to deal very honestly with words and with people, because they are both alive."

September 29, 1907

It's the same old place. (University library.) As I write the afternoon sun strikes through the high west windows, and lies in long light across the study tables. Over on the other side of the room some fellows with green eye-shades are beginning to turn on the electric lights. Across the table here a Tri-Delt in a long brown veil is flirting with a smooth-browed freshman, and the girls at the Pi Phi table are surreptitiously passing a bag of salted peanuts around. Miss Compton stares "unseeingly" into space and the four o'clock gong has just stopped sounding.

As for me, I read for an hour in "Who's Who in America," striving to obtain more information which will make me appear "well read" at the teachers' meeting in McCook. After that I found Whitman and read those thundering outcries of his "for the fibre of things, and for inherent men and women."

How his demands ring in the heart after one has finished reading and seeing the words:

"To stand the cold or heat—to take good aim with a gun—to sail a boat—to manage horses—to beget superb children—

"To speak readily and clearly—to feel at home among common people—

And to hold our own in terrible positions on land and sea."

When one calls to mind the spirit, the "image" of some other poets' poetry, say Tennyson's, how crude and wild and elemental and instinctive and frank and wholesomely free Whitman seems; almost savage in his crudeness, yet full of the Truth about life; the high priest of the cleanliness and beauty of the fundamental and primitive. When one puts the book away on the shelf, what comes to one is from the German,—"es lebe das Leben,"—which, being interpreted, is "Let life live." . . .

No, it is never in the "saying" that I find fault with Walt, but rather perhaps in the proportion of his values. If Walt felt that way, bless you, there is no reason why he should not say so. Let us say the truth, by all means, and if we do not like to say the truth as it stands, then let us make the truth something we can like to say. . . .

But while, as I say, I like Walt's love of "the great uneducated man," his love of "the single leaves of grass," his love of "the children of Adam,"—I do not wish to marry Walt. . . . You could not *give* him away to me for a comrade. . . . Any picture of him will show that there was always a button off his vest! (Yes, he wore vests.)

January 17, 1908

10

Feelings and Emotions

A few more excerpts will serve to indicate her emotional alertness to the people and things about her, and the range and sensitivity of her feelings—characteristics that were conspicuous even in her early childhood. Perhaps they also give hints of the nature of the "themes" she might have "developed" had she not become straightway intrigued by the social and psychological problems of human happiness. These claimed her almost undivided attention after she had begun her own graduate and professional life. But by that time she had begun to create issues, movements, and viewpoints, rather than simple and personal "themes."

The alliance of her literary gifts with the projects of "Young Science," whose advent she had already heralded in her verse and in her letters, conspired then to make her clearly the most influential of the women in her field of work. This influence was supported, furthermore, by her own emotional vivacity and sincerity, which gave her remarks a firmness and an earnestness, always tempered, however, by a lively humor and a critical justice.

She could animate a class of inert high-school pupils into staying after school to discuss the structure of the eye. She could equally easily, and more than once did, enliven a lay conference or a meeting of school superintendents so that they also would linger over time to ponder "the selection of leaders," or "education for democracy," or "individual differences," or "the curriculum for bright children."

In an obituary notice in the *Teachers College Record* a colleague recorded that "(her) inexhaustible interest in human beings coupled with her capacity for fun endeared her to people of all ages.... Her sense of humor was prodigious; nine out of ten of her social acquaintances declared her to be the wittiest person they knew."

Whenever I stand under trees on a silent autumn day I find myself listening as the leaves flutter down, half-expecting some outcry as they flutter, but none ever comes. And again and again this thought recurs: How even the leaves shame us in their mute submission to the Laws of Life.

That I should even expect a protest shows in me that everlasting human "resistance," human imperfection of sight, human lack of transcendent faith. Did I ever tell you before that places are always thinking? Well, they are, and the most thoughtful places in all the world are autumn landscapes, for into them has passed the great consciousness of the naturalness of death and quiet faith in the completeness of the Laws that made us and use us, and return us to the earth again. Fall is my best beloved time of the year.

October 1, 1906

My sole comment is . . . give me Ethelbert Nevin and his melody. For when he calls a story of his "A Love Song" he makes it true with harmonious chords, rich with undertones, loving with melody and sacred with prayerful minors. When he plays of "A Star" this music has one shining golden heart from which scales radiate in twinkling beams. When he says "Good Night" there is tender phrasing, there are deep-toned broken chords, and strangely sweet notes beating, like the sound of heart on heart.

Oh . . . they say that men who have made "mere melody" do not "live" as long as they of the vast, composed inharmonies; but as long as I live I pray that the Nevins may live too. Whether they are great or not does not matter.

January 9, 1907

Professor S. wrote a beautiful letter. As I read it I thought again of how kind and loyal he was to me through all those four college years, and my soul rises up and calls him blessed. It was he who gave me a "paying position," declared my fitness for seminar courses, pruned down my registration blanks, lent me umbrellas when I forgot my own or lost it, and it was he who taught me many lessons in the wisdom of life, and showed me what it means "to stand all day by the roadside, And be a friend to man."

March 13, 1907

Well, tonight three of us teachers went out over the twenty-one tracks, past the busy round-house and over burnt grass, till we found the Republican River. Then we sat down beside its gentle flowing and "rested from the labors of the day." Over on the farthest bank everything was in yellow. Had one been painting the picture upon canvas one would have used dull chromes, brilliant orange, pale canary and cobalt with sienna in it. And for the shadows in the background one would have used cool raw-umber, with a possible touch of crimson lake. We came back very hungry, very tired. I am still tired, so no more tonight. Tomorrow I will "tell you all."

October, 1907

Miss N. gave me a copy of Sargent's "Prophets," that noble, wonderfully conceived frieze. Tonight I sat for a long time looking at it. With what majesty that "goodly fellowship" stands forth! And in their gazing eyes one sees all "the burden of the desert."

In the middle Moses stands, with the two giant tables of The Law. On one side goes Elijah, mantleless, and on the other side Joshua grasps his sword and scabbard. In a long-robed group of three walk Haggai, Malachi and Zachariah, and behind them Micah turns away his face in despair, because "the good man is perished out of the earth."

Next to him comes Daniel, bearing a lettered scroll in both his hands, his face emaciated with mortifying of the flesh; and Ezekiel stands beside him, silent and stern-eyed. Nahum is there in a robe black as darkness, and with uplifted arm upbraids Nineveh. But Amos leans stolidly on his staff, and with his steady eyes implores the people to "Harken unto this word."

So the procession moves on through the list. Under his cowl the earnest face of Habakkuk looks forth, and one thinks with uplifted heart of the "Prayer of Habakkuk the prophet upon Shigionoth." Isaiah steps in front of all the others and with outstretched arms cries "Woe unto the land shadowing with wings," and when one looks at the thin face and deep-set eyes of Jeremiah one is not surprised to remember that "word came unto Jeremiah from the Lord."

Truly this great picture is wonderfully made. One can look at it a very long time, and the mind does not weary.

September 26, 1907

Today by express a little parcel started toward you. In it are two of my best-beloved pictures, both having for the central figure the sweet, clear face of the loving Christ: Christ speaking gently to the unseeing Nicodemus; and Christ, the child, questioning the Doctors in the temple. . . . Not till after they had packed the pictures did I reflect that I had bought them because *I* liked them.

December 22, 1907

Take for instance "The Song of the Lark" which hangs in a gallery in Chicago. Outside the gallery walk seethe the living men and women, but I would leave them any day to enter and look at that other human soul *living* through the canvas. There steps the peasant girl, bare-footed, with her sickle in her hand. Behind her rises, red with light, the harvest moon. And in her alert young body, her upthrown head, the suspended sickle, one hears the song of the lark clear and free rising from the wheat fields. And one's "spirit" is up-borne.

May 28, 1908

I love greatly, and almost above all, those pictures of intangible things, the mist, the wind, the sound of water, the tenderness in the attitude of young mothers. Some man had made a representation of "Omar's Rose." . . . If you were an artist with that task before you, how would you set about it?

For me, I would paint the moldered grave "of some dead Caesar" and over it the blood red "rose," rioting and *living*, with burning heart bared generously to the winds and heats and dews of earth; with its strong roots clinging to the rich ground; with its passionate blossoms flinging their brief life unsparingly forth in perfume and color; not niggardly nor fearful because they must perish, and that soon; unmindful of the dead beneath them; mocking the paleness of death and the human struggle after immortality; loving the earth that feeds them; not aspiring far towards the sky beyond their reach; existing for the joy of their hour. . . . But probably one could not paint all that into a red rose vine.

January, 1908

Religion as a phenomenon has interested me greatly, especially in the last few years. I can remember no "struggle with orthodoxy." I think I was never afflicted with it. I wished to know how men found out about the "Father, Son and Holy Ghost" and no one was ever able to get down to the "basic idea" for me. So I concluded that the whole thing was man-made, and that, so far as I could discover, God had never spoken.

July, 1906

But I think I see The Law in fragments only, and that is why I cannot but feel the oppressive burden of "the broken-hearted and them that sit in darkness and in the shadow of death."

August, 1906

Yet to me there is not in all history any spirit so lovable as that of the man Jesus.

January, 1908

I can well imagine that the "message" of Westminster might well be "the dignity and reality of spirit." In looking upon memorials and the works of these same poets one is overcome by that feeling of conviction, and I should think it would come to one in the presence of their "dust." Whenever I think of the poets and the "apparent" unrealness of their chosen and beloved values, I always think of a line from O'Shaughnessy's Ode,—

> We are the music makers
> And we are the makers of dreams . . .
> Yet we are the movers and shakers
> Of the world forever, it seems.

Think of them! Those lovable spirits, with their faith in the beauty and truth of their "dream." Surely their faith is justified and the power of their "dream" proved. Why else should they have "inherited eternal life?"

July 26, 1908

Finally I shall give again a quotation from one of the earliest of her letters, a quotation that has already been used more than once in my records of her as an emblem of the life and personality of Leta Stetter Hollingworth.

As for me, I think I could care above all things to have my life absorbed by human beings, just to give as much as I have to *people*. I believe that they are as willing and eager to absorb one's life as lawns are, or kettles or hats. I conceive of it as terrible to lie at the end of the world on one's death-bed, and look back upon rows and rows of shining kettles or "good investments" or medicine bottles emptied in the interests of one's "health." I have that sinking feeling when I think of it. Such things seem to me so pitifully futile, but there is more comfort in the thought of life being absorbed by life again. So I should prefer to give what I have to human beings, since give it somewhere we all must.

August 19, 1906

11

An Interlude and Marriage

For the next five years there was a pause in the development of the professional interests of Leta Stetter. This interlude was occasioned by the fact that she had married an impecunious graduate student, not yet quite through with his Ph.D. requirements and poorly supplied with revenue for the support of two people.

The risk of this economic situation was taken deliberately on both sides after long waiting and thoughtful consideration of the hazards of the future. Even after the husband should have his professional degree, there was no certainty of an appointment. Openings in the field of psychology were scarce in those days. But both of the young folks, now twenty-eight and twenty-two years of age, wanted to be together. If possible, they wanted a period of companionship in the East and at a great university before being located, perhaps for life, in some remote place with no memories in common save those from the Nebraska days. Through expediences which for several summers kept the young man profitably employed, while also travelling in Europe, it looked as if resources for at least a year were in sight. And so they were married—yes, and lived happily ever after.

When the degree was conferred on Leta Stetter's husband in May, 1909, he was appointed to an instructorship in the university where he had just completed his graduate work. The appointment was as instructor of psychology and logic in Barnard College, Columbia University. In time, after annual reappointments, he became a permanent member of the faculty. But the first five years were hard sledding. Rigorous economy was required, for the $1,000 initial salary was slow in increasing and at first only the most urgent needs could be met, and these only cautiously and by joint effort. The story of this struggle for a foothold

An Interlude and Marriage   73

for a place in the field of science and scholarship may be told elsewhere, and need not be rehearsed here.

During the earlier years of married life Leta Stetter Hollingworth's time and energy were chiefly consumed by housework, cooking, dressmaking, mending, washing, ironing, making her own hats and suits and endless other domestic duties in the frugal apartment home. Almost always she effectually stifled her own eager longing for intellectual activity like that of her husband. Day after day, and many long evenings, she led her solitary life in the meagerly furnished quarters, while he was away at regular duties or seizing on this and that opportunity to earn a few dollars on the side, by lectures, tutoring and assorted odd jobs not usually included in the career of a "scholar."

"Staying at home eating a lone pork chop" was the way she sometimes facetiously described her experience in these days. There were occasional periods of discouragement; once in a while she would unexpectedly and for no apparent cause burst into tears. These slips from her customary determined and courageous procedure she could hardly explain then, even to herself. Later she was able to make it clear that it was because she could hardly bear, with her own good mind and professional training and experience, not to be able to contribute to the joint welfare more than the simple manual activities that occupied her.

Alternatives were earnestly enough sought. Teaching appeared ruled out, for married women were not given appointments in the schools of New York. In odd moments she tried again to write the kind of thing that she had always declared would interest her—short stories on themes other than illicit love. And as she had long before predicted, these things found no ready market. Occasionally, for her own pleasure, she wrote verse again. A few of these poems have been preserved and are reproduced in a later chapter. They were written, it seems clear enough, after her marriage, but there is no way of dating any of them more accurately than this.

After the first year or two it became possible to include in the budget a "tuition" item, that met the cost of enrolling for some courses in the graduate school. These were at first still chosen in the general field of literature, but they were irregular, more or less unrelated, and seemed little calculated to promote professional skill in writing. They were, in fact, just such courses as her earlier teachers had said they would be, and were full of "dry bones."

Hoping that things might develop more constructively if she could carry a full program of work, she applied for various scholarships and fellowships, but with no success. What she had to offer seemed nowhere to be what was wanted. This was in fact to be her history for much of her life endeavor. For her actual work, at any designated responsibility, she was always rewarded with promotion and due compensation. But she was never successful, as many appear easily enough to be, in enlisting the aid of any of the social agencies, foundations, or institutions in any original enterprise of hers, however significant.

No one will ever know what she might have accomplished for human welfare, always her dominant motive, if some of the sponsorship freely poured out on many a scholarly dullard had been made available for her own projects. She could always join endowed "committees" which could then evaporate along with the endowment; and after this had happened she then often took the work into her own hands. In this way failures were made to yield results that might later be pointed to with pride, and confused with the activities of the languishing "committee." But as an individual worker her best research received little or no "societal" encouragement, and it was usually conducted on her own slender resources. This result was foreshadowed in the futile attempts to secure "remission of tuition" in the early period of her training.

Toward the end of this period Leta Stetter Hollingworth began to consider seriously the goals of education and numerous problems of social maladjustment that she had encountered or observed. She resolved, when it became possible for her to finance a more extended program of study and training, to leave the general field of literature and to specialize in education and sociology.

She enrolled as a candidate for the master's degree and in June, 1913, received the degree of Master of Arts from Columbia University; at the same time she was given, by Teachers College, the Master's Diploma in Education, which certified "the satisfactory completion of a course of professional study for Teaching and Educational Psychology."

This first step in her new professional aim was not suddenly achieved. Her "registration book" shows that in 1911–12 she completed the first course (Education 222, E. L. Thorndike). In 1912–13 the courses she managed to pursue were Educational Sociology (Suzzalo), Sociology (Giddings), Psychology (Krueger), and Education (Thorndike).

In the three following years, as she continued her work for the Ph.D. degree, she carried further courses in Education and Sociology, her instructors being Giddings, Monroe, Thorndike, Kilpatrick, McVannel, Ruger, and Shenton. But the work for the M.A. degree was completed in 1913. She presented for her master's essay a piece of experimental work that subsequently grew into her Ph.D. dissertation.

12

Clinical Psychology Begins

At about the time of receiving her M.A. degree, the opportunity arose to serve as substitute in the administration of mental tests (Binet, Goddard, Terman) in a clinic for mental defectives. She took this place during the temporary absence of Emily T. Burr who had begun it as one of the earliest workers in this field. Leta Stetter Hollingworth had never used these tests which had been newly devised. But on hearing of this temporary part-time work, which could be carried in addition to her housework and might be an opening wedge into a field of professional activity, she speedily trained herself in the use of the tests, and took the job. So adequately did she fill this post that when the original worker returned from her temporary absence, both were retained for the work in the clinic. Of this episode she once wrote:

> Dr. Max G. Schlapp had just returned from Paris and wished to introduce Binet's methods into his Clinic for Mental Defectives. I, who had prepared myself for work in schools, found myself working in a hospital—a great surprise to me.

In the following year (1914) the psychological examiners giving mental tests were put under Civil Service supervision, and positions of this sort, having quickly justified their existence, began to increase in number. Competitive examinations to establish an eligibility list were held in the following spring. The first position as psychologist under the Civil Service in New York was thus established, and Leta Stetter Hollingworth, heading the list, was appointed to fill it. Of this experience she wrote the following brief account:

> In 1914 the City of New York established the first position for psychologist in the Civil Service, and I was appointed to fill this

then unique post. When I was transferred to the Psycopathic Service, at Bellevue Hospital in 1915, Dr. Menas S. Gregory, then head of the Service, said to me, "And what do you do?"

I answered, "I am a psychologist." "And what is that?" "I give mental tests." This conversation shows how new mental tests were at that time.

Immediately Dr. Gregory set me to work in his private office, "to see for himself" what I could do. He did not scorn me because he did not know about my techniques. He listened and learned. He saw the value of the new methods and created a laboratory of psychology within his Service. He was and is one of the most open-minded and progressive officers of public welfare that New York City has ever had.

As a clinical and consulting psychologist Leta Stetter Hollingworth achieved exceptional prestige. She was skillful and effective in establishing rapport with those with whom she worked, whether patients or members of the staff. In those days, cooperation of the members of the jealously guarded medical profession was often more difficult to secure than cooperation of the patients to be examined. Along with this fine sense of personal relations, so important in those dealing with other personalities, she had a keen sense of scientific precision and caution, and abominated slovenly work in any field. Combined with these her own psychological insight, already evidenced in her work as a teacher, and her rare gift of expressing her results and interpreting her observations, made her work as a clinician unusually valuable.

She was rapidly advanced in this field as assistants began to multiply and the usefulness of this kind of work became increasingly apparent. A most complimentary proposal to make her chief of a psychological laboratory to be established in Bellevue Hospital, with prospects of rapid development and far-ranging usefulness was extended to her at about the time she completed work for the Ph.D. degree in 1916, and it was with expressed reluctance that the authorities received her decision to accept instead another opportunity that had been opened for her, in Columbia University.

Activities as a psychological examiner and consultant were by no means limited to duties in the hospital clinics. Most cases there dealt with were referred by the courts or by various social and charitable agencies, or sometimes by the school authorities. They were likely to be delinquents, or dependents, or misfits of some sort that had come to social attention. Cases soon began to be referred to her by individual physicians and educators, parents, school administrators, lawyers, and sometimes to come of their own accord, for her guidance and advice. Outside of regular hours she quickly built up a busy round of activities in the psychological and educational guidance of individual children and adults. Work of this sort developed so rapidly that it soon overtaxed her time, and she could easily enough have dropped her clinical connections and occupied her full time as a consulting psychologist. There was in her approach to these relationships a sympathetic and understanding confidence and a courageous attitude that induced in her clients an affectionate faith in her wisdom, a belief in her findings, and a willingness to follow her counsel. Year after year many of these people returned, or wrote to her, to report on their progress or to thank her for her assistance, or to send others to her for similar professional advice. I have estimated that she served as intimate psychological adviser, during her lifetime, to at least four or five thousand distressed individuals.

The predominant contribution offered by clinical psychology in those days seemed to be the study of the mentally backward and deficient. These were the cases that most often came to the courts and to the clinics. These were the ones that were most obvious cases of educational maladjustment, and the ones about whom parents and guardians were most likely to feel concern. "The bright can take care of themselves" seemed to be the tacit assumption, and it was not until later years that the chief interest of Leta Stetter Hollingworth, as an individual psychologist, focused itself primarily on those whom she considered more "favorable deviates."

She was particularly active in these days in helping in the organization of societies for the study of mental defectives, and in gathering together for the discussion of professional ethics and responsibilities the small group of workers then entering the field of clinical psychology. She was also vigorous in her defence of the professional status of such workers, and especially active in campaigns to achieve for them legal recognition, institutional respect, standards of training and preparation, and recognition, at the hands of the highly organized medical men, of their qualifications as technical specialists.

She appeared before hospital boards, boards of education, before the state legislature, and before various commissions; she consulted with the governors of at least two states in these interests. Psychological examiners came to turn to her at once for advice and direction when in their own particular situations they experienced difficulties in making themselves understood or in getting the cooperation they needed. She threw herself into these campaigns with all the intrepidity and vigor that were so characteristic of her whenever she became convinced of the justice of a cause in a field in which she felt herself competent to know and to speak.

But of no less importance than these professional considerations, appeared to her the opportunities offered by the new methods of studying in a more scientific way than had ever before been possible, the educational and social problems growing out of the varieties of human endowment and the complexities of social relationships. Immediately she began to study the records and data accumulating in the clinic files, and to publish papers on the results of these analyses. Before she received her Ph.D. degree in 1916 she had published a half dozen scientific papers, chiefly in the *Medical Record* and in the *American Journal of Sociology*. These publications can best be considered after reviewing her further graduate work.

13

A Doctor of Philosophy

It has already been noted that on receipt of her M.A. degree Leta S. Hollingworth continued to pursue courses and other requirements leading to the degree of Ph.D. in Teachers College, Columbia University. The master's essay which she submitted in 1913 was further developed, and had in fact been but a preliminary report of progress in a major series of experiments she had under way. She proceeded to bring this work promptly to a close and to publish it as a number in the *Teachers College Contributions to Education* two years before her formal requirements for the degree had been recorded.

There is at hand a receipt from the Bureau of Publications, dated June 17, 1914, acknowledging the payment of $125 as "part payment of bill for printing dissertation." Later than this come, in the collection of documents found among her papers, the Civil Service notices, reports of her standing in the eligibility list, and of her appointment as psychologist.

Dated March 14, 1915, right in the middle of these competitive Civil Service examinations, is a note "from the Committee," signed by Henry Suzzallo, notifying her that she has been "exempted from the preliminary examinations in the fundamental fields of history, philosophy and psychology of education," and admonishing her, "You will however report to your major professor for the preliminary examination in the field of your research interest."

Dated January 12, 1916, is an inquiry from the Registrar concerning the record of the fulfillment of "the language requirements for the Doctor's degree." On February 4, the Department of Sociology writes accepting the course in Social Psychology as "one of the eight courses required for the double minor in Sociology."

February 8, 1916, the Registrar reports "your successful examination in your major field for the Ph.D. degree, which examination was held in June, 1915."

A "Roster of Examinations, Doctor of Philosophy, Faculty of Philosophy" is preserved, setting the date for her oral examination as eleven o'clock, Saturday, May 13. Other candidates, scheduled for such examinations in the same division on this roster, were Thomas R. Garth, Lorle I. Stecher, Mabel L. Robinson, William A. McCall, H. J. Sheridan and Clifford Woody. And dated May 15 is a note from the Secretary of the Dean of the Graduate School reporting "your successful examination for the degree of Doctor of Philosophy," and "enclosing your registration book for your souvenir collection."

There is also a copy of the bill from the Bureau of Publications, dated May 31, 1916, stating the additional amount due on the printing of the dissertation (total $322.64). There was later some merriment over the terms of this publication contract, and as other examples accrued, occasional well-meant and fully deserved sarcasm about its "fiduciary aspects." For instead of receiving credit on each copy sold, the author was presented with additional bills.

The diploma, recording admission of Leta S. Hollingworth to the degree of Doctor of Philosophy, is dated June 7, 1916. It is signed by the no doubt wearied hands of the Dean and the President, but as an indication of the progressive note in education it is written and printed not in Latin but in English.

14

Poems Written in Adult Life

The shift from the general literature of nature and of human relations to the more factual subjects of sociology and education, in the activity and in part in the interest of Leta S. Hollingworth, was a notable change in the outward aspects of her development. Although she had written in one of her earlier verses that

> *God has never spoken since mankind*
> *Let go fair, flashing fancy and seized thought.*

this did not deter her from the cultivation of a more empirical outlook, nor from the adoption of the experimental method. In fact, in a brief autobiography which she was asked to write, and to reply to the question how she came to be included in the list of women of achievement in that album, she wrote, in conclusion:

> I do not know. I was intellectually curious. I worked hard, was honest except for those minor benign chicaneries which are occasionally necessary when authority is stupid, disliked waste, and was never afraid to undertake an experiment or to change my mind. My family motto, translated from the Latin, reads, *I Love to Test*. Perhaps that is the explanation.

At any rate, this was one of the points in her career when, so far as overt activity was concerned, she changed her outlook. She turned away from "testing" the ready-made sentences that had long run through her mind to another kind of testing—not only the measurement of human abilities, but also putting nature to the test, searching for new relations and probing into the status of alleged truths.

After this point she wrote, so far as is known, no more short stories. There remains a group of seven poems, in the collection already referred to. These, as internal evidence indicates, were written in the years after her marriage. They represent her last writing of this character, although she never lost interest in general literature, and always had a special enthusiasm for poetry, of which she read much. She developed many close friendships, particularly with a number of women who were writing. Since her later work and the bulk of her publications are in so different a direction, these few poems are reproduced here, before the account of her scientific researches.

THE BRIDE AND THE RING

Oh, we must be dear friends, little ring,
Through all days and winds and weather,
For some day you and I, little ring,
Must lodge in a grave that the years will bring,
  Together.

Must lodge in a grave? You and I?
Nay, Christ, nay! That cannot be!
But a strange, dim woman, faded and old,
And a strange, thin, worn little band of gold,—
  Not we!

THE COURTESANS

We were the courtesans of ancient Greece.
Nor time nor death can lull our hearts to peace.
Our hearts, once flaming with that subtle sin
Of women who will neither weave nor spin.

Half-stifled from those ranks of matrons fair,
That served the looms, we burst away! Undone!
Shame stricken, forth we fared; while there
With bated hearts and muted breath they spun.

Outcast, but free, we went, with skirts that flowed,
And took the body's rhythm in the breeze.
Sappho was of us, and Aspasia bode
With us as one, and with her Pericles!

We watched the flocking boats wing out to sea.
The skies of Greece burned wide upon our gaze.
Dream-taught, we conjured up a prophecy
That brightened word by word, till in amaze

We glimpsed a vision on the sands dim brown,—
All women, walking free, within the town!
We were the courtesans of ancient Greece;
Nor time nor death can lull our hearts to peace.

PRAIRIE LOVE

I love you as I love the strength of wings
That bear the hawk up even with the sun,
And hold it floating at a height that none
Unwinged may reach. So, sure and strong it flings
Itself into the ether. Thin, bright things
That form from vapor hover on that flight.
The fires of heaven burn more redly there,
When sunset kindles. In that far blue air
Soars rapture. So your love with light
Strong pinions holds me to the height.

THY LOVE TO ME IS AS THE STRENGTH OF WINGS*

Thy love to me is as the strength of wings
That bear a bird up even with the sun
And hold it floating at a height that none
Unwinged may reach. There, seraph-like, it sings
For the pure love of singing. Thin, bright things
That form from vapor hover on that flight,
And great sounds shout that mutter down on earth.

I love thee as I love the strength of wings!
Oh, my beloved, when I see swift birds
Fleeing along the clouds, those spirit-words
Cry thro' me, and I listen, and up springs
Yearning, and hope, and nameless faith that sings.

*A modified form of the preceding verse.

REMEMBERING

Last eve a wandering wind
Passed over the grass and me.
I marvelled, but did not find
A reason why it should be
As though a kind hand stroked my face.

Yet my blood grew quick in me.
Then, all on a sudden I knew!
That evening—the first that we
Kissed each other,—a little wind blew
Over us, long ago, in another place.

I HAVE HEARD SONG

In the hot night when everything is still,
And on the sleepless eyeballs looms the square
The dull gray window makes, and everywhere
Life flickers, speaks a whisper stern and chill,
That seems the listening silences to fill—
"Thou too must find the grave": I think on these:
I have heard song,—I even heard a lark
Sing on a barren grave,—and seen the trees
Bear fruit; and after deep black dark
Seen dawn; and felt the swift sea breeze
Salty as life blood; loved white butterflies;
Watched Autumn flush the silent, solemn land;
And I have felt my hand within thy hand,
And known thee wonderful, and found thee wise.

THY LETTERS

I read in many an old and famous book
How many warrior heroes perished, crying
That love had taught them not to shrink from dying,
And felt this to be great. Lately I took
Thy letters, love, thy tedious absence giving
Me no peace, and read them thro' and thro',
And as I read, a greater love I knew,—
Thy love, which taught me not to shrink from living.

15

Early Research and Publications

The dissertation presented in partial fulfillment of the requirements for the Doctor's degree was a report of an experimental inquiry into some of the alleged limitations experienced by women in the use of their abilities. In fact the subject of several of the earlier scientific studies by Leta S. Hollingworth had for their aim the further clarification of problems felt by her to exist in connection with the social status of women. Her very earliest observations of ordinary family life had shown her that although frontier women undertook their due share of the burden of life, and this in addition to their distinctly feminine reproductive functions, they usually had little control or authority over the course of that life.

She found in addition a strong social tendency, in literature, in romantic paintings, and in the institution of chivalry, as well as in religiously propagated ideals and conventions of conduct, to emphasize the role of women in the historic domestic pattern. It seemed to her unlikely that woman had by original nature, in all cases and inevitably, interests that were to be best satisfied by conformity to this pattern, and she wished for all individuals the greatest amount of personal freedom consonant with the general good.

Moreover, she found specific handicaps interposed in the way of deviation from the domestic pattern, on the part of women. Institutional rules, and sometimes laws, offered such obstructions. Women were not allowed to vote; they must assume their husbands' names; they could not be appointed to various jobs; when they did find work, it was usually for a smaller stipend, not because their work was less valuable, but because they were women.

The rolls of achievement and the lists of eminent people, in nearly every walk of life, it had to be admitted, included chiefly men. At the same time, the institutions for the feebleminded also had more men than women inmates. Sons appeared to be regarded as more valuable than daughters; she often made use of an illustration drawn from a letter of inquiry received by the psychologists at the University in her early years there. This letter read as follows:

> I hear that there is a possibility of having tests made for vocational guidance.
> We have three children, two daughters and a son; and naturally we are greatly interested in his career. Would it be possible for us to have him tested at your laboratory?
> Awaiting a reply, I am.
>
> etc.

She fretted at the barriers interposed in the way of her own pursuit of interests, but this fretting was for her more than a subjective tantrum. It immediately issued in an endeavor to see just what the facts were, and on what conceivable grounds the social status of women had come to be what it was. And why had they so inferior a record in the halls of fame? So she set about reading all that she could find on the subject of "men and women." She found plenty of material, mostly written by men, to be sure, and most of it "armchair" scribbling or mere benevolent chatter or beguiling flattery. Among the alleged reasons for the relative inferiority of the work of women, and the excuses for the barriers quite generally encountered by them, she found such things as the following assertions.

Women are actually inferior in their abilities to men, and should be treated accordingly.

Women have just as "good" abilities as men, but these talents lie all in the direction of sympathy, tenderness, nursing, child care, decoration, and the like.

Women are primarily and biologically chiefly sex objects, and their primary role is and ought to be based on their reproductive function. At most they should merely serve as interesting companions to men.

Women, by virtue of the rhythm of their menstrual functions, experience regularly recurring interferences with the use of all their abilities, and must be considered for a considerable part of each lunar period as invalids, or semi-invalids.

Women as a species are less variable among themselves than are men; all women are pretty much alike but men range enormously in their talents and defects. This was used to explain at the same time the greater frequency of men in the lists of distinguished people, and also their greater frequency in institutions for the feeble-minded.

Every one of these armchair dogmas she questioned. She determined to submit them, one after another, to searching examination and investigation and at least to learn the truth about them. She had already served as assistant director, with her husband, in an experimental study of the effect of caffeine on mental and motor abilities. Interestingly enough, one of the precautions taken by the experimenters, in this study, in their zeal to control all of the possible variables, was to have the women subjects record the occurrence of the menses, during the six week experimental period. It was considered possible that this physiological process might have some complicating effect on the records, so that at least the item should be taken account of.

She found that when the data from this investigation were reported, no results were attributed to this event in the work of the women subjects. Upon studying the data for herself she found no evidence that there was any variation in performance associated with it. And she reasoned that here was a way to put this old dogma to the test.

So for herself she set about a new experimental investigation, using both men and women as subjects. The experimental variable was the presence or absence of menstrual activity. Using an array of laboratory measurements of speed, accuracy, steadiness, and covering both motor and more strictly mental activities, she drew the work curves of her subjects and tried to discover therein variations in performance that could be correlated with "functional periodicity."

She found no evidence of the alleged "rhythms" that were supposed to appear in such work. So far as the processes included in her own study were concerned, and as a matter of fact therefore in the only experimentally conceived study of the matter, no such necessary rhythms occurred; the "cycle" of performance declared by others to exist "is not discovered by methods of precision." The concluding paragraph of this monograph, after a calm but merciless comparison of the experimental outcome with the armchair dogmas, and some consideration of the probable motivation of the latter, is as follows:

> It seems appropriate and desirable that women should investigate these matters experimentally, now that the opportunity for training and research is open. Thus, in time, may be written a psychology of women based on truth, not on opinion; on precise, not

on anecdotal evidence; on accurate data rather than on remnants of magic. Thus may scientific light be cast upon the question so widely discussed at present and for several decades past,—whether women may at last contribute their best intellectual effort toward human progress, or whether it will be expedient for them to remain in the future as they have remained in the past, the matrix from which proceed the dynamic agents of society.

There is in the exultant ring of this closing declaration a note that shows clearly enough why Leta S. Hollingworth had been willing to "let go fair, flashing fancy, and seize thought." It might well be that God would never speak, through these techniques, but the human soul could speak thereby, and here was a way, perhaps, of "painting the Universe *as it is*." Here was a way for the people to learn to follow Truth, rather than Magic. One is so vividly reminded of the letter she wrote while still a high-school teacher, a letter that has already been quoted:

> Sometimes I almost shake with the joy of thinking that I live in *this* day of the world, and that before I die I shall see the coming of a new religion, which is to touch the hearts of all the hungering people through Science and Scientists.
>
> November 18, 1908

She had found the answer, perhaps, to a question she had raised in a letter written just after her Commencement Day at the University of Nebraska:

> Will it ever be possible for any man to step forth from the influences of his own *types,* and interpret the Universe *as it is?*
>
> September 20, 1906

At any rate from that day forth the weapons wielded by Leta S. Hollingworth were the instruments of science. And she was dauntless in their use, yet wielded them always with a grace and charm that effectually placated and soothed the adversary. Nor did she care whether or not the results conformed to her *type*. For she had already taken her stand on this point:

> Let us say the truth, by all means, and if we do not like to say the truth as it stands, let us make the truth something we can like to say.
>
> January 17, 1908

The scientific papers* that had appeared from her hand before the publication of this dissertation or close to the date of it, were six in number. All of them might be said to deal first of all with the same general issue,—the psychological factors involved in the social status of women. In most of these papers she was blasting away the last foothold of the anti-feminists,—the dogma of the inherent greater variability of the male.

In the first paper, on "The Frequency of Amentia as Related to Sex," she showed, by an analysis of data from institutions and cases passing through the Clinic for Mental Defectives, that "a female with a mental age of 6 years survives in society about as well as a male with a mental age of 10 or 11 years." Males will therefore more often be brought to the clinic, if their mental age is below 10; and they will more often be sent to institutions; but outside such institutions will survive an equal number of equally feeble-minded females.

> The greater frequency of amentia among males has come to be rather commonly credited and is sometimes cited as a proof of the greater variability of males. But all the facts gleaned from these data point to the conclusion that if social pressure had applied equally to male and female, enough additional females would have come to the Clearing House to equal the males. The figures are certainly sufficient to suggest that if our social habit and organization ever change so that sex is no longer of commercial and economic value to women and so that women become mentally competitive to the same extent as men, the number of females in institutions for the feeble-minded will be materially increased.

The second paper, entitled "Variability as Related to Sex Differences in Achievement (A Critique)," comprises an attempt to review briefly data at present accessible as to the comparative variability of the sexes in mental traits, and to discuss critically the hypothesis that the great difference between the sexes in intellectual achievement and eminence is due to the inherently greater variability of the males.

The data thus surveyed were shown to be inadequate and contradic-

---

*Since a complete bibliography is available in the January, 1941, number of *Teachers College Record*, no citation of the numerous articles shortly to be briefly summarized is given here. All of them can be located by reference to that bibliography, which is reproduced at the end of this book.

tory. And even had greater male variability been shown, it would not follow that it was "inherent." And under any circumstances—

> ... it is undesirable to seek for the cause of sex differences in eminence in ultimate and obscure affective and intellectual differences until we have exhausted as a cause the known, obvious, and inescapable fact that women bear and rear the children, and that this has had as an inevitable sequence the occupation of housekeeping, a field where eminence is not possible.
>
> It is desirable, for both the enrichment of society and the peace of individuals, that women may find a way to vary from the mode, as men do, and yet procreate. Such a course is at present hindered by individual prejudice, poverty, and the enactment of legal measures.
>
> But public expectation will slowly change, as the conditions that generated the expectation have already changed, and in another century the solution to this problem will have been found.

In a paper on "An Economic and Social Study of Feeble-minded Women" a study was made of the activities of the large number of women who, though as defective as the males in institutions, were left at large in society. It was shown by the study of a large array of cases what social loss and destruction and what individual misery were occasioned by this difference in the incidence of social pressures on the two sexes.

In collaboration with Helen Montague, M.D., an elaborate collection was made of ten physical measurements of 2,000 infants at birth, and a study of the relative variability among the two groups, boys and girls, was made, in order to secure data as early as possible, before social pressures and "expectation" had an opportunity to mould the individuals. Confessedly, such results would relate only to physical measurements, and it is explicitly warned against the practice of drawing any inferences from physical measurements to mental traits.

> Our results, showing that there is no inherent difference in anatomical variability, suggest that there will be found to be no inherent difference in mental variability, but they do not *prove* that such is the case. . . .
>
> In view of the fact that the most accurate and comprehensive studies so far made of comparative anatomical variability of the sexes fail to reveal any sign of greater male variability, and since there is no experimental or statistical data extant which prove the

greater mental variability of males, it would seem necessary to abandon greater male variability as an ingenious explanation of sex differences in achievement and as the source of "social and practical consequences of the widest significance."

The next paper on "The Mentally Defective as Cases in the Courts of New York City" was one of the earlier studies of the relationship between intelligence level and delinquency; it urged in the light of the findings, a better understanding of the mental endowment of youth brought before tribunals of justice, and the substitution of such understanding for simple punishment and detention.

In numerous papers of later years the psychological factors involved in the social status of women were returned to. In 1916 she wrote a chapter on "The Vocational Aptitudes of Women," for a textbook on vocational psychology. In the same year appeared in the *American Journal of Sociology* a much read paper on "Social Devices for Impelling Women to Bear and Rear Children," and in *The Scientific Monthly* a joint paper with Robert Lowie on "Science and Feminism." The next paper to appear specifically on these issues was in 1922, under the title "Differential Action upon the Sexes of Forces Which Tend to Segregate the Feebleminded." In October, 1927, *Current History Magazine* published an article by her on "The New Woman in the Making," and in 1929 she contributed to the 14th Edition of the Encyclopedia Britannica the article on "The Psychology of the Family."

Although articles on the social psychology of women no longer appeared in her bibliography, she by no means abandoned her interest in that theme. Instead, she began planning a large-scale ventilation of the whole topic, in a volume which she had planned to entitle "Mrs. Pilgrim's Progress." She had in part outlined the contents of such a volume, had saved many clippings and much other relevant material, but always had to postpone it as more urgent things appeared. The world never allowed Leta S. Hollingworth to forget that she was a woman, and she in turn never wholly abandoned her original project to depict the long and tortuous path of Mrs. Pilgrim's progress. But this project was left incomplete, and it can never be finished by another hand.

Although Leta S. Hollingworth's interest in the cause of the freedom of women was scientifically motivated, and her material appeared in the technical journals, she was at once hailed by the "feminist" group of women in New York as the much needed scientific pillar for the cause. In the *New York Times Magazine* of September 19, 1915, she was given a full page write-up by Rheta Childe Dorr, under the title "Is Woman Biologically Barred from Success?" A detailed account was there given of her origin, her education, her marriage, her housekeeping, her struggle for professional training, and the series of conclusions from her papers on the psychological factors involved in the social status of women. In her own quiet way, Leta S. Hollingworth took her stand with this group of liberal although somewhat more agitated women. In the early days of the "Woman's Movement" she and her husband marched together in the "suffrage parades," along with many other university people. She often gave oral accounts of her findings and their meaning to dinner clubs and discussion groups in the city. She became an active member of "Heterodoxy," a group of lively and intellectual professional women in the city who met periodically for discussions of current issues and their group interests, and was a member of this group as long as she lived. Many of her best friends in the East were made in these ways. Among her papers, dated October 31, 1917, was a Certificate designating her as Watcher for the Woman's Suffrage Party, to attend the polling place in the 29th Election District of the 22nd Assembly District in the City of New York.

Another turn in the affairs of Leta S. Hollingworth came immediately after she received the Ph.D. degree from Columbia University in 1916. She was then offered the post of Instructor in Educational Psychology, in Teachers College of that university. If she accepted, she was to take up the work formerly carried by Naomi Norsworthy who had just died. This was particularly the field of the psychology of exceptional children.

She hesitated a long time before making up her mind which course to pursue, for she had also just been offered the position as Director of the Psychological Laboratory to be established in connection with the Psychiatric Service at Bellevue Hospital, where she was then employed. She decided, finally, in favor of the educational rather than the clinical field, and in this work at Teachers College she was engaged for the remainder of her life.

16

A Home at Last

For the earlier half of her life Leta Stetter was homeless, in the permanent sense of that concept. At the age of two or three, when her mother died, she was taken with her sisters to live with the maternal grandparents in the cabin on the White River. When this temporary retreat was broken up, a stepmother was on the scene and the children were taken to live with their father and his new mate. These were the days of the "fiery furnace." The two adults were seldom at peace; twice they were united and twice separated. For various periods during these years the children lived in the home of an uncle, where they were welcomed and kindly treated. This uncle became, in fact, a sort of paternal surrogate in the feelings of Leta Stetter and she cherished a life-long affection for the members of this family. Their residence and the simple frontier shelters of the grandparents came as close to feeling like home as anything she was to know in her childhood. "There's no place like home—thank God!" she once wrote.

After she left Valentine for college at the age of sixteen she followed the typical student practice of the shifting domicile—first in a boarding house, then in a faculty home, then with sorority sisters in rented chapter houses that changed at least twice while she was still in Nebraska. Through college and the succeeding years she enjoyed the friendship of Nellie B. Pickup and her sister who lived together in Lincoln. Mrs. Pickup was a fellow reader in the English Department at the university and the sister was an active business woman. On frequent friendly occasions and in any emergency the Pickup home was a welcome retreat, and the letters of Leta Stetter richly reveal the happy anchorage and the deep affection which the homeless student found with these two loyal friends. The bonds of friendship here established endured throughout the lives of those who met there and it was my good fortune often to be one of these.

If there is any place that is less a city of homes than New York it must be a disconsolate spot. Many inhabitants of that city have no first-hand understanding of the meaning of home other than that derived from peripatetic apartment life. New York has few spots in which homes in any other sense are possible. For those not economically well situated the box-like tenement arrangements are even less home-like than a Pullman car, and it was in such quarters that Leta Stetter Hollingworth and her husband lived in their earlier years after she went to New York. Six different apartments, two hotels, and a rented rural parsonage in turn became their alleged home before they were able to move to the country and establish a haven that was their own.

This place, finally known as "Hollywyck" was built as a summer home in 1916, the year in which Leta Stetter Hollingworth was appointed to the staff of Teachers College, and in 1932 it was expanded and rebuilt into a year-round dwelling. Only in the last seven years of her life, therefore, was Leta Stetter Hollingworth privileged to live in a place that would accommodate her every need and interest, that was flexible enough to become an expression of her own ideas and tastes, and gracious enough to be a reasonably fitting background for her versatile activities. She became much attached to this place and often expressed in conversation and in her letters her delight in it. It was at "Hollywyck" that she lived in the last and most strenuous period of her life, a period in which living so far from her place of work perhaps induced occasional conflicts between her love of her home and the urgent demands of attendance upon duty.

"Hollywyck" is located 38 miles north of the city, in a wooded territory in a broad bend of the Hudson River. Half a dozen Columbia professors had bought up the region, composed of parts of two or three old farms that had become thickly covered with second-growth timber, with many old oaks, hemlocks, hickories, chestnuts, and tulip trees surviving and a dense crop of new saplings of many species. There were dogwoods in profusion, elm, several varieties of birch, ash, butternut, iron wood, maple, poplar, spruce, pine, sycamore and myriads of hemlocks, in addition to the older trees, and here and there an old apple or cherry tree. Here these families had built up country estates of six to ten rocky acres each, and the remaining land was held for latecomers. The colony was only a short walk from the New York Central station of the village of Montrose and three miles from the considerable town of Peekskill.

The colony was surrounded by rugged foothill country, and in early years deer, foxes, and numerous small animals were in the woods. Surrounding two sides of the colony was a forest reserve, several square miles in area, which soon became the Blue Mountain Reservation, a Westchester County Park area, with miles of footpaths and equestrian trails, three lakes and many small streams. The colony was thus securely private and secluded, protected on all sides from undesirable encroachments. It was close enough to civilization to be within easy commuting distance from the city yet wild enough to seem like a section of the Catskills. It thus combined in a most unusual way the advantages of both urban and forest life, with few of the disadvantages. As time went on the colony expanded by the growth of families and the addition of new colonists, most of whom were psychologists associated with the university and all good friends. During the later years fourteen families comprised the colony.

This spot had been chosen after much exploration of the regions outside New York City as the best place to found a final home for the two New Yorkers born in Nebraska. A small acreage was secured, which was later expanded. A simple but commodious structure was built, and this served for many years as a summer retreat which still made possible summer session duties at the university. When by 1932 city life had become intolerable even in winter, the original structure was made over into a fourteen-room house, with bountiful provision for work, play, ordinary living, books, help, guests, and pets. No architect's prejudices were solicited. The house was constructed around the psychological needs of human beings, not according to the traditions of any deceased dynasty. Where buffers were desired, either for eye or ear, they were forthwith erected, with little consideration of how they would appear in a photograph. Any part of the house could be effectually shut off from any other section, yet remain easy of entrance and exit. Two living rooms, a study, dining room, kitchen, laundry, telephone room, coatroom, foyer, numerous closets, three pantries, six bathrooms, two stairways and six bedrooms, each provided with desks and bookcases as well, made up the interior arrangement. In a separate building extra provision was made for a small family, for a shop, for storage, and for five cars. There were two fireplaces, an ample basement, adequate heat and water, a tennis court, gardens, terraces, lawns, and all around the native woods. Within sight but hardly within hearing in all directions lived choice friends.

Until her professional duties became too burdensome and her energy strangely depleted, Leta Stetter Hollingworth derived the deepest joy from the development and use of "Hollywyck." She gave her special attention to indoor furnishings and arrangements, leaving outdoor developments mainly in the hands of her restless husband. But the outdoors was also one of her chief pleasures. She walked, played tennis, skated, coasted, chopped faggots, and unceasingly photographed special objects, corners and people, finally turning to motion photography. Most of the photographic and film records now available, of the place, its people, their friends, and their activities, were taken by her hand.

Here she freely brought her friends, from the city and from the West: able people in whom she was interested; protegés whose progress she wished to facilitate; colleagues for conversation and clients for consultation when this last could not be avoided; neighbors for a social occasion; a bridge club for an afternoon of relaxation; and often the whole colony for a tennis tournament or some other kind of get-together.

Among the notable features of the colony was the strong individualism and passion for privacy of most of its members. So long as they felt like it, no one bothered anyone else. But there were occasions when one family might bring all the others together, like housewarmings whenever a new member joined the group and other celebrations and community activities. Leta Stetter Hollingworth was more gregarious than most of the individuals in the group, and when she could manage the time for it she was always eager to take part in a social enterprise. She did this with an easy grace and an unfailing charm and thus comfortably compensated for the more reclusive and introvert inclinations of her husband. She often expressed her surprise, upon rejoining a group after a few minutes absence from it: "You are funny," she would say to her husband. "So long as I'm there you never say a word. Then when I suddenly come back I find you active and talkative. You can and do talk interestingly. Why don't you do it when I'm there too?"

The remark reflects the eager animation with which she readily entered into social contacts, and when it was appropriate she could become the center of a conversational group. Among her characteristics most frequently remarked by those who knew her best were her zest, her enthusiasm, her friendliness, her courage, her cogency, her wit, and her understanding. These traits were easily made noticeable by her quick intelligence, her resolute purposiveness, her passion for the beautiful, her devotion to the truth, her remarkable command of verbal expression, and her adherence to the ideals of integrity and loyalty that had been hers since childhood.

It was in the free play of her intellectual and emotional life during the final years when she was the personal inspiration of a real home that many of these traits ripened into full maturity. It was then that she most clearly revealed to all who knew her what eternal springs of insight, of vigor, and of tenderness had brought her through the ordeals of an unhappy childhood to the precious influences and the steady achievements of maturity.

In her absence "Hollywyck" is an empty shell, its rooms are bare and dead. All the features solicitously put there for contented human relations stand like heavy monuments to the brevity of life. Often enough they seem even to whisper of the folly of hope and of the futility of aspiration. Only in the memories of those who loved her remain the evidence that belie these ominous voices and challenge their bitter whispers.

> Enclosed is a leaf from a dogwood tree which I brought home from last Sunday's adventures (at Hollywyck). I still think of the amazing beauty of that place and wonder how it's possible that it belongs to us. . . . The dogwoods were brilliant red, which made the hemlocks look brilliant green. The yellow birch leaves had all fallen, and lay in a deep carpet under all the trees. The sunset was a rose-colored fire, burning between the branches of the big hemlock. As the sun went down the moon came out and poured a cool, bright light over everything. That lasted all night long.
> After we went to bed things were perfectly still for quite a long time. Then an owl began to hoot softly in the woods. One got the strongest feeling of magic's being, after all, true and real. In the morning the sky was overcast. It was a gray day. We went for a walk all around the lake, the girls all looking for building sites for themselves, and finding them, as we went. In the afternoon it rained and we built a nice fire in the fireplace and sat around it contentedly till it was time for (us) to go to the train. . . .
> Doesn't the place seem unreal to you now (in your absence)? Like a beautiful wish-fulfillment, existent only in daydreams? Strange that our lives and all our belongings should be as beautiful as the day-dreams of other people are, and as our own once were.
> October, 1918

> Walking down to the post office in the heat of the summer sun I experience the old-time thrill at finding letters. . . . The souvenir

of leaves redintegrates my home completely—my heavenly home, which with characteristic caution I have achieved while still on earth, not trusting to the problematic future. I see the gold and green of the landscape in the evening sun. I sense the peace and beauty of the house. From this distance, under the influence of redintegrations from the environment of my 'teens, my home . . . seems like a wonderful dream, so perfect that it could never possibly be realized.

August, 1926

17

At Teachers College Columbia University

Acting Dean Paul Monroe, "by the authority of the Trustees" forwarded to Leta S. Hollingworth on August 10, 1916, an appointment as "Principal of School for Exceptional Children and Instructor in Educational Psychology," from September 20, 1916, to June 30, 1917. This school for exceptional children, the direction of which was to be part of her work as then planned, was a short-lived project. As a tuition school it was to have accommodated the backward children of well-to-do parents with both pedagogical and medical attention or supervision. The building that had been secured for the purpose did not conform to the fire laws for schools, and other complications arose, so that the College soon discontinued this enterprise.

The following year full time was given to instruction in Teachers College, chiefly in general educational psychology and the psychology of exceptional children, and the appointment for this year read simply "Instructor in Educational Psychology." Appointment to teach in the summer session of 1917 followed, and for most of the next twenty-two years Leta S. Hollingworth was on duty in Teachers College summers as well as during the regular session.

In a communication dated April 11, 1919, she was informed by the Dean, with congratulations, of her promotion to the rank of Assistant Professor of Education on and after July 1, 1919. On September 26 of the same year, continuing her affiliation with clinical psychology, she was also certified as Examiner in Mental Defect by the New York State Commission for Mental Defectives.

She became Associate Professor, beginning with the year 1922–23. In 1928 she was promoted to a full Professorship, beginning July 1, 1929, and retained this position to the end of her period of service. Compensation in this part of the University did not conform to the schedules adopted and recorded in other parts of the institution, but remained more or less on a negotiation basis. As the years went on there were also salary cuts, which were never wholly restored, so that as her work became better and better known and her influence increased her income steadily dwindled. Intimations that the allowance provided for her work was incommensurate with the prestige conferred by that work on her institution were always met by her with the declaration that "for the present it is enough that Mrs. Pilgrim is afforded an opportunity to carry on her work."

During the earlier years at Teachers College she continued to spend at least one day each week in the Psychopathic Service at Bellevue Hospital. In 1921, under the auspices of the Neurological Institute of New York City, a Classification Clinic was organized for "Physical and Psychological Examination of Adolescents." Each of various specialties was represented in the personnel of the clinic, which was directed by Pearce Bailey, M.D., and Sanger Brown II, M.D. At the annual meeting of the Trustees of the Neurological Institute, December 13, 1921, Leta Stetter Hollingworth was appointed Psychologist of the Classification Clinic. This was an expensive clinic and the "fee for examination and opinion" was announced as "$200 paid in advance."

In 1922 another collateral appointment occurred, this time to give a course in Educational Psychology at the New School for Social Research, in a special and endowed program for adult education there organized. Numerous other formal appointments were received from time to time. As a matter of fact, and it produced a good deal of merriment at the time, she once received notice from municipal authorities that she had been appointed "physical examiner of police" in New York City. Of course she quickly repudiated this appointment, which was presumably due to some administrative or clerical vagary. She served also from time to time on examination boards for the city school system, in connection with lists for mental examiners, inspectors of ungraded classes, and the like.

In 1939 she was assigned to a seat in the Faculty of Philosophy of Columbia University, and to the Division of Educational Research in Teachers College. About two years earlier she had been designated representative of Teachers College, in charge of research, in Speyer School (P.S. 500), jointly established for a five-year experimental period by the College and the Board of Education of New York City. It was to be an experimental school for the study of educational problems of exceptional children, especially "slow learners" and "rapid learners," but excluding the mentally deficient.

So much for the more or less official aspects of her connections with Teachers College and Columbia University. With this chronological outline in mind attention may now be devoted to the more intrinsic features of her work subsequent to her appointment to the teaching staff of Teachers College in 1916, upon the suggestion and recommendation of Professor E. L. Thorndike.

The tiny triangular shaped cubbyhole into which Leta S. Hollingworth first carried her materials when she began her work in the overcrowded halls of Teachers College, remained for twenty-four years a topic of jest and expostulation for students, parents, visiting educators and foreign dignitaries who wanted to interview her. There was barely room for a desk, a couple of filing cabinets, a tiny set of bookshelves, and a chair. Often enough the visitor would have to be interviewed in the hallway outside, because some other person was sitting in the chair in the office, and when this was the case, the office was "fully occupied." It was necessary for her to alternate occupancy of the room whenever she had a part-time assistant to help her with the papers and records of the hundreds of students who would be in her classes at a given time. There was no way for two people to work in that place.

Nevertheless thousands of people thronged to that office, not only students in great numbers, but fully as many "outsiders." For many years she continued to hold consultations of a clinical and advisory sort. For some years nominal fees were charged for this work; half of the amounts thus received the College appropriated; the other half she was then allowed to devote to research purposes. There are available copies of detailed and precise reports of the use of such funds. As time went on she became wholly unable to devote any attention to these individual consultations, and from time to time she vigorously advocated the establishment in the College of a well equipped Guidance Laboratory, for such public and educational services. As the years went by, such a Guidance Laboratory was finally achieved, and special personnel designated for its work.

Since no other rooms were available, all her research activities, as well as data, had also to be squeezed into Room 334, Macy Hall, her tiny "office." After she had instituted projects in experimental education in the city schools, and wished to follow up the development of the children there studied, sometimes by annual or more frequent interviews, over a period of twenty years or more, all these individuals had also to meet her in this little space. She often came home with amazed stories of the sumptuous quarters for research and office accommodation and assistance provided for the staff of smaller institutions to which she had been invited to conduct conferences and series of lectures. It does not follow that any more would have been achieved by her had the college halls been more ample. This institution has never yet achieved adequate housing for its amazingly productive staff, and the volume of "contributions to education" that has poured from that busy center of educational training and research continues to astonish people in sister institutions which are able to provide lavish quarters, with good illumination, research rooms, private offices and full-time assistants, and even with "research funds."

18

Courses of Instruction and Books

A survey of the courses of instruction offered in Teachers College by Leta S. Hollingworth during her period there as an Instructor and Professor, reveals about ten main projects. In addition to these courses, developed by herself in her own program, she cooperated in various other courses.

One of these fields was General Educational Psychology. For some years she handled a section of this large course, in which most of the major students registered at one time or another in the course of their work. She spent a great deal of time mastering the fundamental principles of human psychology and their relation to education, and collected a great variety of apt illustrations and examples for use in this course. This more theoretical field was, however, not the one she most enjoyed, and she had relatively little interest in the abstract disputes over systematic issues in psychology, or over the more philosophical riddles often made much of in such general courses. She found the principles elaborated by E. L. Thorndike adequate for the analysis of the work of the teacher and the problems of the learner, and was content to move on to the practical application of these principles, with little or no worry over their reconciliation with various "isms" that might arise from time to time.

Before long more special fields in which she was working developed and courses multiplied, so that in time she was relieved of complete responsibility for one of these general sections. But she continued to participate in various ways. From time to time she gave sets of lectures in such courses as "Psychology Today." She also developed a general course dealing with psychology for nurses, and gave this not only in Teachers College but also at Bellevue Hospital. And when the educational program of candidates for the higher degrees was modified so as to include one major course in "Foundations of Education," given jointly by various members of the staff, she regularly represented psychology in one or more of the sections of this fundamental course. She never undertook to write a general textbook of educational psychology, all of her volumes being on more restricted fields. She did however cooperate with others in the production of a mimeographed outline or summary in connection with the course in Foundations of Education. She was also appointed Adviser in connection with the instruction of nurses in a hospital in Brooklyn and made occasional trips there for conferences or brief talks.

Another enterprise in the general field in which she always participated was the Seminar. This was a meeting of several members of the staff and of the advanced research students, for the purpose of reviewing and guiding current researches undertaken by the candidates for the Ph.D. degree. This actual meeting was but a gesture, as compared with the great amount of time required for the individual guidance of students sponsored by herself, or on whose doctoral committees she was designated. Countless hours had to be spent advising, planning, arranging for research facilities and materials, reading the manuscripts submitted, re-reading them when revised, and finally attending the oral examinations, and perhaps assisting to edit the manuscript when the dissertation was printed. At one time, in order to introduce some system into these burdensome duties, she gave a research course for those working in her special fields, and thus tried to see them more often and keep in closer touch with their projects and plans. A list will be given of the research projects of such advanced students for whom she was official sponsor or adviser.

List of Dissertations since 1920 sponsored by Leta S. Hollingworth or for which she served as chairman of committee. (Provided by Registrar of Teachers College.)

BENNETT, ANNETTE G.—"A Comparative Study of Subnormal Children in the Elementary Grades." (1932)

BERE, MAY—"A Comparative Study of the Mental Capacity of Children of Foreign Parentage." (1924)

BLAIR, GLENN M.—"Mentally Superior and Inferior Children of Junior and Senior High School Age." (1938)

COLLMANN, ROBIN D.—"Psychogalvanic Reactions of Exceptional and Normal Children." (1931)
CRUMP, BONNIE L.—"The Educability of Indian Children in Reservation Schools." (1932)
DUNLOP, FLORENCE SARA—"Subsequent Careers of Nonacademic Boys." (1935)
DUROST, WALTER N.—"Childrens' Collecting Activity Related to Social Factors." (1932)
GRAVES, KATHARINE B.—"The Influence of Specialized Training on Tests of General Intelligence." (1924)
GRAY, HOWARD A.—"Some Factors in the Undergraduate Careers of Young College Students, with Particular Reference to Columbia and Barnard Colleges." (1930)
LAMSON, EDNA E.—"A Study of Young Gifted Children in Senior High School." (1930)
MCHALE, KATHRYN—"Comparative Psychology and Hygiene of the Overweight Child." (1926)
MOORE, MARGARET WHITESIDE—"A Study of Young High School Graduates." (1933)
O'CONNOR, ZENA C.—"The Runaway Boy in the Correctional School." (1938)
PARTRIDGE, E. DEALTON—"Leadership Among Adolescent Boys." (1934)
PORTENIER, LILLIAN G.—"Pupils of Low Mentality in High School." (1933)
PRITCHARD, MIRIAM C.—"The Mechanical Ability of Subnormal Boys." (1936)
ROSEN, ESTHER K.—"A Comparison of the Intellectual and Educational Status of Neurotic and Normal Children in the Public Schools." (1925)
RUST, METTA M.—"The Effect of Resistance on Intelligence Test Scores of Young Children." (1931)
SICHA, MARY HUNTER—"A Comparison of the Rorschach 'Erlebnis-Typus' of Comparable White and Negro Subjects." (1939)
SIMPSON, MARGARETE—"Parent Preferences of Young Children." (1935)
SPENCER, W. DOUGLAS—"The Fulcra of Conflict: A New Approach to Personality Measurement." (1938)
TIRAPEGUI, LUIS A.—"Comparative Variability in Anthropometric Traits of Normal and Feeble-minded." (1924)

VANUXEM, MARY—"Education of Feeble-minded Women." (1925)
CONKLIN, AGNES M.—"Failures of Highly Intelligent Children." (1939)
SIMMONS, RACHEL MCKNIGHT—"A Study of a Group of Children of Exceptionally High Intelligence Quotient in Situations Partaking of the Nature of Suggestion." (1939)
SCOTT, WINIFRED S.—"A Study of Reaction-Time of Intellectual Deviates." (1939)

In addition to the foregoing completed studies, three others under her sponsorship, in whole or in part, are still in progress.

One of the first of the more special courses to be developed by her was the one on "Subnormal Children," which she inherited directly from her predecessor, Professor Naomi Norsworthy. Her work in the clinical field, predominantly concerned with feeble-minded children and adults, had richly prepared her for this course, and she had an abundance of material, in the way of typical cases, and much experience with their identification, measurement, treatment and education. This course continued to be given throughout her service at Teachers College, and in connection with it grew up various relations, such as those with the department of ungraded classes, in New York City's school system. She served also as adviser, on the faculty, of those students preparing for work as teachers or supervisors of ungraded classes and backward children.

In 1920 the materials as given in this course up to that time were brought together in a volume, *The Psychology of Subnormal Children*. This fundamental text was reprinted nearly every year thereafter up to at least 1930. It was dedicated to "Elizabeth E. Farrell, A Pioneer in the Field of Which It Treats," a good friend of hers who had for years been in charge of the department of special classes in the New York City school system. The text was addressed primarily to teachers, rather than to clinicians, and the illustrative material related to the achievement of such children, rather than to their physique or their clinical features. A colleague, writing in the *Teachers College Record* after her death in 1939 said of her work in this field:

> Professor Hollingworth's investigations established her early in her career as the leading authority in the psychology and education of subnormal and delinquent children. Her *Psychology of Subnormal Children* has been a standard text since its publication in 1920. She was responsible for the establishment of special classes for subnormal children in many commu-

nities and served as adviser to the officers in charge of this type of education in New York and many other cities, states and foreign nations.

Even before the publication of this general text, a monograph appeared from her hand entitled *The Psychology of Special Disability in Spelling* (1918). This volume reported some of the results of her first major project in experimental education. When the school for exceptional children was abandoned, shortly after her initial appointment to Teachers College, she organized a special project to study school children, not mentally defective, who had special difficulties in certain school subjects.

One of these school subjects was spelling, and this monograph gave an account and analysis of the results of this part of the experiment, a fuller report of which will be given at a later point. It is mentioned here because it was instrumental in determining the character of another course given by her, dealing with school maladjustments in which the primary factor was not that of general intelligence.

This investigation aroused a good deal of interest among educators; the monograph has long since been out of print, and an endeavor to secure second-hand copies was unsuccessful. So far as Leta S. Hollingworth was concerned, the study served to interest her further in general questions about special abilities and disabilities, and a course covering these topics was in time offered by her in the department. This field not only articulated, through its emphasis of disabilities, with the field of general mental deficiency; by its equal emphasis of specialized abilities, it may have been one of the factors that eventually turned her main interest away from the feeble-minded and defective deviates to the highly intelligent, the gifted, and the rapid-learners.

Five years after the appearance of the monograph on Spelling, and just two years after the text on Subnormal Children, there appeared her next volume, a textbook on *Special Talents and Defects*. In this text, after introductory chapters on the neural basis and the relationships among capacities, she considered five main topics—reading, spelling, arithmetic, drawing and music, summarizing the material then available on special ability or disability in these fields. A chapter was also devoted to miscellaneous topics and a final chapter to the problems connected with individuality, its discovery and fostering, and its relation to the problems of education.

Interest in this field was continued, although most of her own energies became directed toward other topics. But as late as 1931, and in a subsequent revision, a well-known *Handbook of Child Psychology* contained two chapters by her, one of these being on "Special Gifts and Special Deficiencies."

The psychology of adolescence is another field in which she began to give instruction from the beginning of her work at the College. In reviewing her work in this connection a colleague summarized it briefly as follows:

> The period of early adolescent transitions, physiological and psychological, appealed to Professor Hollingworth as one of special interest and importance. She offered the basal courses in the psychology of adolescence from the time she joined the staff. She has conducted many studies of her own and sponsored a number of Doctor's dissertations in the field. In 1928 she published *The Psychology of the Adolescent*, which not only immediately became the standard text in the field but also established a new point of view. In this book, adolescence appears to be much less the inexplicable result of inevitable ebbs and flows of physiological and chemical forces than the intelligible outcome of efforts to solve tangible problems of adjustment. Two chapters, "Psychological Weaning" and "Finding the Self" have become classics of psychological literature.

This volume on *The Psychology of the Adolescent* also aroused considerable interest abroad. Sections of it were reprinted in one of the German periodicals. The British edition of the book was first requested and was brought out by a London publisher. The *Red Book* magazine ran as an editorial a summary by her of the chapter on "Psychological Weaning," and there were many demands for articles, lectures and conferences, on topics related to youth, outside the college classroom. In this connection, in part, she was appointed a member of the White House Conference, and to various other bodies concerned with our human resources, with problems of youth and social adjustment, and she prepared numerous careful memoranda for the use of such bodies. Much of her private consultation came also to be with young people and parents, on problems of family relationship and other matters becoming more or less acute at the time of adolescence. At the time of her death she was on the point of bringing out a revised edition of this volume, which the publishers had been urging upon her for several years. The *Handbook of Child Psychology* also contained a chapter by her on this period of development.

Quite early in her teaching career she proposed and organized a new course, called "Mental Adjustments." She conceived that most difficulties of personal life had an educational basis. Either the individual was misinformed, or misguided, or wrongly trained, or other people, such as his parents, guardians, teachers, required enlightenment, and perhaps adjustments of their own. Furthermore, many maladjustments were themselves in connection with school problems, school plans, or vocational aims. Including all these themes within the sweep of the discussion, she elaborated in this course what might be called her philosophy of the healthy mental life. This included individual matters, social relations, family adjustments, psychopathology when this had a functional basis.

Leta S. Hollingworth lived and worked in a period of history when much attention was being given to mental hygiene, psychoneuroses, and psychotherapeutic methods and theories. In her day cults of all kinds, including healing cults, flourished and the greatest varieties of interpretation of the vagaries of the human spirit were ventilated. She based her own interpretations and methods on the sound principles of normal psychology, especially on the principles of learning. She was asked to write, for a subsidized volume on *The Problem of Mental Disorder*, a chapter on "Education," an illuminating chapter which has been much read and also reprinted. There she undertook to show how much mental disorder is a direct outcome of faulty learning, in much the same way that the experimental animal may acquire bizarre and inutile habits in trying to find his way out of a maze or puzzle box. Experimental confirmation of this generalization has been forthcoming in psychological literature since this chapter was written. Of this contribution a colleague wrote:

> During a period characterized by conflicts and extravagance of theory, Professor Hollingworth's practice and writings, distinguished as they were by astuteness, soundness, and integrity of judgment, contributed greatly in bringing order out of threatened chaos.

Among other courses to which she gave special attention was one on Clinical Psychology. This was a training course for those planning to enter the field of clinical work, in which she had herself had so many years of experience. In this course she endeavored to teach the approved methods and procedures, studied with the class typical cases from her files, and encouraged each student in the detailed study of one or more individuals. As clinical methods developed so rapidly and many others entered this field, it became less feasible for any one individual to cover the topic in a brief course, away from an actual clinic. This course was therefore dropped and in time was supplanted by the more elaborate provisions of the Educational Clinic or Guidance Laboratory established in the College. In spite of her early and long experience in the clinical field, it is to be noted that Leta S. Hollingworth never showed any interest in devising any "new test." Her greater interest was always in putting to the best possible use such methods as were at the time available.

She participated in courses on The Psychology of the Family; on Mental Development; and in various Demonstration courses, in which she herself examined a child before the audience of students; and she was throughout associated with such courses as were instituted for the training of teachers in special schools and classes for the handicapped, or for the bright.

The subject to which Leta S. Hollingworth, as the years went on, came to bring her maximum zeal and enthusiasm was that of intellectual giftedness in children. It is true that when she first went to Teachers College in 1916 and undertook to explore the field called "exceptional children," the word "exceptional" was almost a synonym, in educational discussions, with "backward." Classes for backward children were indeed often called "special opportunity" classes, although she and others working in education soon came to give this term a different meaning. Her actual experience, moreover, in the clinical field had been chiefly with the handicapped.

Nevertheless, one of the very first papers she published after her appointment to Teachers College was the description of an unusually intelligent child, discovered and demonstrated before this class concerned with "the exceptional." In almost the same month that she published her paper on "Echolalia in Idiots" appeared also this paper on "The Psychology of a Prodigious Child," in which she had the cooperation of two of the child's teachers.

From that time on her interest in the gifted as distinguished from the backward rapidly developed, until her own projects in experimental education dealt exclusively with these "favorable deviates." Even that early we find her declaring:

> Science has already furnished us with a means of identifying exceptional children, and of measuring the amount of their exceptionality, so far as intelligence is concerned. If science within the next fifty years should furnish us with the means of prophesying adult achievement on the basis of the child's exceptionality, the history of human progress might be modified in ways of which we

now can but vaguely guess. We should then be able to select and cherish human genius without regard to race, sex or condition of economic servitude.

Beginning with this declaration in 1917, it was in a very real sense that she mapped out the cause to which she was to dedicate the very best efforts of the rest of her life. It was in this cause, the identification and fostering of our very best natural resources, our bright children, that she came to be best known not only in her own country, but the world over. In a later chapter evidence is submitted to indicate the truly international range of the influence of her work with gifted children.

But material on the gifted was scarce; few had yet been identified. In California an important study of these exceptionally bright children was under way, and awakening great interest through the enthusiasm and genius of L. M. Terman. Here and there others were expressing an interest in the problems of the gifted child, just as for many years there had been an interest in adults displaying genius.

Beginning with 1922, a series of studies began to flow from her pen, reporting chiefly her own observations, experiments and reflections. These culminated first in her volume, *Gifted Children,* which was published in 1926, almost in the middle of her career at Teachers College. In the second place, these studies led later to the establishment of an even more carefully planned series of educational experiments, in which she was engaged at the time of her death. In 1942, two and a half years after her death, a volume on which she had been at work for many years was completed by her husband and published with the assistance of the Carnegie Corporation. It is *Children Above 180 I.Q.*

This brief survey of her work as a teacher in the University, and of the courses to which she devoted herself there, may well terminate with a statement made in an account of her written by a colleague in the *Teachers College Record.*

> Professor Hollingworth's influence on the general pattern of psychological work has been as great as her contributions to areas of specialization. When she entered the field, psychology, in the main, was a study of abstract facts and principles. One could read a "child psychology" from cover to cover without encountering a child or feeling the pulse of human life.
> For her, psychology became a source of tools, methods and techniques for further understanding of a human being. The relative validities of traditional psychological abstractions, problems of mind-body relationships, and the squabbles among the "systems" interested her little. No psycholo-

gist of her generation has more clearly and consistently made his work the study of "the whole child."

(Her) work with exceptional children gave expression to the fundamental traits of her character and her personality. Her decisions and opinions were based on facts; she was opposed to all forms of educational wishful thinking. Although she was always impervious to the appeal of sheer sentimentality, she was capable of the deepest affection for human beings and intense devotion to human welfare.

The subjects of her studies were never human guinea pigs to her; they were the individual objects of her deepest concern. She remained on intimate terms with all the members of her various experimental groups of gifted children, visiting them, encouraging and advising them, and in a great many cases supplying tangible necessities for years of further education.... This intense interest in and devotion to the living individual, combined with the clear-eyed vision of the scientist, accounts for the unique scientific validity and practical value of her contribution.

19

First Educational Experiment

Three successive projects may be described as constituting the major experimental enterprises of Leta S. Hollingworth in the distinctive field of education. The first of these is the one-year analytic and remedial program with children deficient in particular school subjects. This experiment was carried on during her first year at the College, 1916–17, with the aid of two special teachers. The pupils were selected from Public School 192, Manhattan, and they met for special teaching periods in such rooms as could be made use of at the College. There was one class for poor spellers (Miss Winford) and one for pupils poor in arithmetic (Miss Keator). Leta S. Hollingworth "was responsible for the psychological analyses and for the planning of specific experiments and . . . for the conclusions set forth in (the) report." E. L. Thorndike and F. G. Bonser "gave much time and thought" also to the project.

The project itself is described in the Preface of the monograph *Special Disability in Spelling* as follows:

> We wished (1) to observe, over a considerable period of time, the learning of pupils with special pedagogical defects, i.e., those pupils who are of normal general capacity, but who are incompetent in one particular school subject; (2) to apply psychological tests to such pupils, with a view to a diagnosis of their disabilities; and (3) to discover and devise, if might be, remedies for such defects. Incidentally we wished also to study the psychological processes involved in mastering the two school subjects, arithmetic and spelling.

The general procedure is given in the following (abbreviated) outline:

1. To teach spelling by a great variety of devices intended to make the subject interesting. . . .

2. To become personally well acquainted with each child, and to note physical and temperamental difficulties which might conceivably contribute to failure in spelling.

3. To measure quantitatively the improvement of the group, and of individuals, under special instruction.

4. To carry out group experiments in the psychology of spelling, with special reference to the factors involved in failure.

5. To study each child by means of psychological tests, with special reference to diagnosis of his deficiencies.

6. To look for some means of removing the causes of failure.

So far as the spelling project is concerned, "The children in the Arithmetic class were used as controls in measuring improvement under instruction, etc."

The precise results of this analysis of good and poor spelling and of good and poor spellers are too technical to summarize here, and it required the monograph of over 100 pages to set them forth. For the present purpose it is enough to refer to that monograph and to point to certain characteristics of the general aim of the experiment. The project and its report throw as much light on Leta S. Hollingworth as they do on the process of spelling. Spelling was, to be sure, to be taught, and group experiments were to be made. But the dominant aim as expressed was one that characterized all of her research work in later years. It was the emphasis, not of the mass results, the group scores, or the statistical averages purporting to portray some hypothetical person. Instead, it was the emphasis of *the individual*. The aim was "to become well acquainted with each child," "to study each child," and this "with special reference to *his* deficiencies," and finally, "to look for means of removing the causes of failure."

Leta S. Hollingworth put herself on record more than once, especially in some of her addresses to groups of educators and research workers, as having little use for studies in which individuals were submerged in an array of statistics. She held up to high scorn many of the procedures of investigation current in her day.

"It has become a fashion," she once declared, "in educational research to rush forth hastily with a huge load of pencil and paper tests; to spend an hour or two on a hundred children; to rush hastily home to the adding machine, there to tabulate the performances of the children, not *one* of which has ever been perceived as an individual child." And again—

"There is a tendency to get away from the individual child in favor of vague masses of children.... I know of investigators of child psychology who would feel that there had been some breach of dignity or of etiquette if he or she had actually sat down and worked with a child. 'Assistants, of course, attend to all that,' is their slogan.... In this way the investigator loses all vital contact with the subject of investigation, gets no live suggestions from watching children react, is at the mercy of such interpretations as his assistants may put upon the reactions made."

Finally, "If an investigator of child psychology can be saved from ever having to manage and observe a child, he can certainly thus avoid much fatigue.... But those who really study children *must* be prepared to 'take pains'."

She had no use for scientific "ghosting" and in her own work never resorted to it. At least one of the results of this policy was that her remarks and conclusions drew always on a wealth of concrete illustration, based on personal experience of the things talked about. This gave her public addresses, for example, a ring of sincerity and an authority that often received comment. Remarks such as the following were often overheard in audiences after some of her speeches:

"Now, there's a woman who knows what she's talking about!"

"There's a woman who has her feet on the ground!"

"Why, she must really *know* those children or else she couldn't talk that way about them!"

The point for the moment is that this insistence on face-to-face contact with the individuals to be studied was not a proceeding arrived at by fumbling, or by trial and error, nor was it an exhortation handed out to others but not embodied in her own work. It was an essential feature of her attitude toward people and toward her own science. It was expressly declared in this, her first experimental approach to the study of special disabilities. It characterized her methods of research for the remainder of her life. She worked always with concrete individuals. She was fully capable of manipulating statistical averages and of handling adding machines; and she did these things when occasion demanded. But she never mistook a hypothetical average for a human being. Her method *was* laborious; it *was* fatiguing; it *did* involve "taking pains." But it was *her* way of trying to "portray the universe *as it is*."

20

The Special Opportunity Class (P. S. 165)

In 1922 a committee of interested persons was formed to organize an experiment in an elementary public school in New York City. Plans were laid "for gathering together . . . a group of children highly endowed mentally, and providing for them so far as possible the educational opportunities that should seem best adapted to their special needs." Jacob S. Theobald, Principal of the School, was chairman. Jane E. Monahan, Assistant Principal, with Margaret V. Cobb and Grace A. Taylor, temporarily resident at Teachers College, and Leta S. Hollingworth were the other members.

Fifty children were studied in this way for a three-year period. The Special Opportunity Class proper contained children whose Intelligence Quotients were over 155. There were also an equal number in a second group with Intelligence Quotients below this point but over 134. These might therefore be said to have comprised a "gifted" and a "highly gifted" group. Data were also secured on children of equal ability who did not take part in the special instruction of these experimental groups, for purposes of comparison.

Two main ideas lay back of this experiment, once these exceptional children and suitable teachers were found. The first was to study the children, in as many ways as possible; their origin, their background and family circumstances, their psychological characteristics, the course of their development, their physical, social, educational, temperamental traits; to study the course of their subsequent growth, their vocational and economic destiny; in general, to find out what kind of creatures bright children are, from where they come and to where they are going.

The second aim was to experiment with curricula, projects and methods of instruction; to test what materials and procedures are most useful for such children, and how these pedagogical features differ from those in most general use for average pupils; if such children can profit, and society gain, if special procedures were introduced into their educational program, such as segregation, enrichment, rapid promotion, self-instruction, and the like.

During the three years of actual teaching and classroom observation all the members of the committee participated, to varying degrees, in the plans and projects. In such cases many people are satisfied by the initial enthusiasm, and interest wanes when the long pull comes. The report of the studies growing out of this project is to be found chiefly in thirty-two papers published by Leta S. Hollingworth in educational journals, and in her volume entitled *Gifted Children.*

Her interest in the members of these classes continued for the remainder of her life. Eighteen years later she was still keeping in touch with these pupils. They were interviewed and measured frequently in various ways. Their traits, interests, and activities were further studied. When they married, the wives or husbands were drawn into the scientific net. In many cases she assumed exceptional responsibility for the career of individuals in the group.

Because of difficulties encountered in the planning and the material support of the project, the classroom features of this experiment did not get on record as it had been hoped they might. The greatest values of the undertaking were in its success in arousing widespread interest in the recognition and education of the gifted, and in its usefulness in providing material for the numerous follow-up studies and psychological inquiries reported in the series of papers referred to.

In time others were enlisted in the conduct of these studies. One or two of the parents of the children became valuable assistants in the follow-up studies. Other educators began to make use of the accumulated test data and measurements. Several of the graduate dissertations sponsored by Leta S. Hollingworth were reports of such follow-up studies, or analyses of the data originally collected. These data are in fact still on file and in active use, especially in studies of the predictive value of early measurements.

Some of the studies in this stream of reports were chiefly valuable in confirming the results of others who had already begun the study of gifted children in other centers of population. But the great majority were on wholly new questions, and their contribution to knowledge in the field of mental endowment was noteworthy. It is of course impossible even to sketch the content of these thirty-two papers resulting from the Public School 165 project in so general an account as this. Such a summary is being provided in another connection, and the papers are all listed in the separate volume giving the complete bibliography of Leta S. Hollingworth.*

Nor is there any possible way of assessing the influence which these papers and other reports have had in stimulating the interest of school authorities and the public in the problems, educational, personal, social, occasioned by the occurrence, in small numbers, of children of these high degrees of intellect. The Board of Superintendents of New York City more than once extended to Leta S. Hollingworth a vote of thanks and appreciation for her work in this and related fields. The most recent acknowledgment has been the proposal to call the Opportunity Classes, now being widely introduced, H Classes, in her memory and honor.

Topics of inquiry with respect to bright children, treated in the series of papers thus resulting were: their size and strength, the intelligence of their siblings, parents and mates, their vocabulary, musical sensitivity, motor speed, neuromuscular capacity, nervousness, discipline, social adaptation, leadership, subsequent growth, personality development, playmates, physical appearance, beauty of features, ability at maturity, rate of growth, later educational accomplishments, family backgrounds, vocational plans and adjustments, honors, special difficulties of personal and social adjustment, profit from special curricular modifications, such as the study of biography, science, and the evolution of common things, and the interrelationships of many of these items.

Achievement of gifted children given the "opportunity" education was compared with that of similar children not so taught. The achievement of the "gifted" and the "highly gifted" groups was compared. Filing cases full of test records and individual data were accumulated and it was planned to continue for so long a time as possible the follow-up study of these children into manhood and womanhood.

In addition to these technical papers, many popular articles on the gifted child were requested, and talks in great number before educational conferences, parents and teachers, clubs, and civic groups were given. To the limit of her time and ability she accepted these invitations

---

Education and the Individual: In Honor of Leta S. Hollingworth, Teachers College Record, Columbia University, December, 1940. Vol. 42, No. 3.

and she often referred to her expeditions to different parts of the country on these missions as "carrying the message to Garcia."

She wrote chapters for handbooks; sections for yearbooks; contributed to the *Proceedings of the First Congress for Mental Hygiene*, was a delegate and contributor to the *White House Conference on Child Welfare*, wrote for the *Annals of the American Academy of Political and Social Science*, and was invited to submit memoranda and proposals to various deliberative bodies and councils. She was, in fact, able to accept but a fraction of the opportunities offered to present her results and ideas about the education of exceptional children in American cities. Of the public addresses, copies or notes of which were found among her papers, about one-third deal with some aspect of the recognition and conservation of the gifted young.

In a Memorandum to the American Council on Education, she wrote that "intellectually gifted children are among the most valuable assets of a civilized nation. To waste them is to waste the fundamentals of power." She persistently pointed out that ". . . the prevailing American philosophy of education favors the weak and mediocre at the expense of the intelligent and the strong."

She lamented the fact that ". . . thus has the word 'Philanthropy' been corrupted to mean love of the dull and vicious."

She did her best to call attention to the folly of the situation in which

> . . . thousands and even millions of dollars are being spent by public education and by privately endowed foundations to identify, study and subsidize the education of delinquents, feeble-minded children, and other biologically unfortunate and socially undesirable deviates. . . . Hardly any of the funds appropriated for public education are directed to the conscious selection or subsidy of the biologically elite.

The vigorous and incisive campaign waged by Leta S. Hollingworth for the educational recognition and the social conservation of gifted children was based on no sentimental platform. It is true that toward such individuals of this sort as she came to know she had a strong personal interest, and she treated them always in their role as individuals, not as "socioeconomic assets." A bright mind at work was to her a spectacle of compelling beauty.

The earlier objects of her passion for beauty were those she found about her at the time—average people, things and natural events. She celebrated these in verse and in story. As life continued she found beauty also in many other things. The activity of human thought, the formulations of science, the instruments of investigation and of proof, the goals of education, the efforts of social behavior, appeared to her in all their loveliest aspects.

Perhaps the most beautiful thing she ever found, which aroused in her a profound esthetic appreciation and therefore commanded her utmost devotion, was the problem-solving dexterity of a bright human mind. So engrossed could she become in the spectacle of a gifted intelligence at work that in her later years the search for such minds and the endeavor to further their appreciation and conservation engaged the greater part of her zeal, both professionally and in her friendly relations. Such minds afforded her the same warm feelings that she found also in form and color, in movement, in human faces, in flowers and clouds, in sea and prairie, and in significant human relations such as those she sometimes captured in her verse. She celebrated them by devoting the rest of her scientific life to their portrayal.

Back of her concern in doing what she personally could for individuals of promise and ability she sensed always the problem of their social value and function. It is to be borne in mind that while still a graduate student, although she majored in education, she elected also a double minor in sociology. Her book on *Gifted Children* is firmly organized so as to lead up to a final trenchant chapter on "Social-economic Implications."

When asked, toward the end of her life, to write a brief autobiographical account to appear in an album of gifted women, this was the topic that above all others stood out in her mind as summing up the trend of her activities:

> I have published four textbooks and parts of others, but the bulk of my writing is in original studies, published in educational and psychological periodicals. There are about eighty of these and they deal for the most part with the psychology and education of highly intelligent and gifted children. I consider this one of the most important of all problems for the development of social science—the problem of how to recognize, how to educate and how to utilize the gifted young.

The final experimental project undertaken by Leta S. Hollingworth, to be described in a following section, dealt also with gifted children. Because of the impetus already given to this topic by earlier work, and the more formal auspices under which the plans were organized, this later project, fourteen years subsequent to the P. S. 165 experiment, received more publicity. It is this project with which her name became so firmly associated in the public press, and it reached a larger audience than did the stream of thirty-two papers and a textbook issuing from its predecessor.

But her own interests and judgments grew definitely out of the less formally organized investigation dating back to 1922. The zealous inquiry into the characteristics and problems of the gifted as individuals received there its initial impetus. The later project, known as Speyer School, or Public School 500, was more or less a tentative fulfillment of this initial drive. It gave an opportunity to develop more adequately under her personal and individual responsibility some of the instructional and curricular problems which had languished in the "co-operative" hands of the earlier committee. But it was seized by the public as if it were some new thing, rather than one on which she and others had been working for a quarter of a century. In one of her reports on the progress of the Speyer School project she recorded that ". . . about fifty scientific studies of the development of highly intelligent children have been added to the literature of education in the years between 1922 and 1938, as a result of the work done at Public School 165, Manhattan."

21

A Tour of Inspection Abroad

In the spring of 1928, Leta S. Hollingworth travelled in Europe, on a sabbatical leave. Although mainly interested in seeing things in general, she was far from forgetting her school interests. She carried with her such letters of introduction, from the University, from the Governor of New York and others, as might give her ready access to special places. The letter from Governor Smith, for example, admitted her, when other resources failed, to the Irish Parliament.

In London she visited with representatives of the London County Council, saw Spearman, Burt Kimmins, and others, and discussed educational problems of common interest, as well as the publication in England of one of her recent books, *Psychology of the Adolescent*.

In Germany she spent a good deal of time visiting the special schools, and schools for the backward and the gifted, both in Hamburg and in Berlin. At each place she bought quantities of such school materials as she found in use, to be used perhaps for demonstration purposes later in her own teaching.

The following pages give brief accounts from her notebook of her observations during six days of visiting the schools in Hamburg and Berlin. Lübeck, the Black Forest, Nürnberg, the Rhine, Scotland, Ireland, London and the English countryside were the main points mapped out in this pilgrimage, but everywhere the schools and educational system claimed an importance that not even a sabbatical year could deny.

Hamburg, Monday, February 27, 1928
    Spent day inspecting *Psychologisches Laboratorium*, talking with Dr. Martha Muchow, and listening to explanation of mental tests and *Auslesung* for the *Oberschulen*. Also visiting the *Oberschulbehörde* (25 Dammtor Str.).

Saw Oberschulrat Dr. Oberdörffer, and obtained permission to visit three of the upper schools. Talked with him of his visit to America next April. Received descriptive literature *in re* reorganization of the schools in Hamburg (see literature).

Hamburg, February 29, Wednesday

1. Visited *Ko-educationsschule,* Vosberg Str. 23, at 9 o'clock. Saw the pupils starting on a Wanderung.

2. Visited *Knabenschule* at Bunderstrasse, and saw English taught. and German.

3. Visited *Mädchenschule* and saw English taught. Pupils seem homogeneous as to ability and orderly in conduct. Also eager to recite.

30–36 pupils in a class. Teachers men in boys' schools. Women in girls' schools. Pupils selected for these schools at 10 years of age.

Hamburg, March 1, 1928

Visited the Museum of Arts and Crafts, which is used in education. Went through the Museum with three different *Wanderungen*—two from boys' school and one from a girls' school. The teachers explained the connection of the old things with contemporary life, and recited the history of the museum pieces. One class had a special "Führer," who recited the history of some of the objects.

Pupils 10–13 years old. Much more self-controlled than American school children. Gave no trouble. Much more homogeneous as to age and size in a class.

Berlin, March 2, 1928

Visited Schulrat Otto Karstädt at the Prussian Ministry of Education, Unter den Linden, 4. Received letters to visit the *Köllnische Gymnasium,* the *Sonderklassen* and *Sonderschulen* (Magistrate Fuchs, 6 Senefelder Strasse) and the Vocational Schools (Dr. Karsen).

Went to the Köllnische Gymnasium and spoke with the Direktor. This is where the *begabten Schüler* are under instruction. Saw a class in mathematics and a class in English. Both good.

Berlin, March 3, 1928

Visited the school for tubercular children (37 Ehrenwald Strasse, Rector Richard Bauer). Saw about 300 children in the open air, in cottages built open to the south.

Tuberculosis of lungs, bones and skin mostly, but of all parts of the body.

Instruction articulates with that of the regular classes. Children attend daily 9–4, in the open air, until discharged by *Schularzt.* On cloudy days they receive *Strahlung* under quartz lamps. Adults also come for this treatment.

Pets, Gardens. Music. Many skin lesions are seen to be healed and healing under the treatment.

Berlin, March 3, 1928

Visited the Shulkindergarten (6 Senefelderstrasse).

These are six-year-olds who legally must be at school, but are not yet *schulreif,* either because of mental weakness or physical weakness.

Thirty children in class.

No reading or writing or formal arithmetic undertaken.

Kept there a year, or perhaps two, if not yet *schulreif.* Must go to regular classes finally, but some go to the *Hilfschulen.*

Each child tested mentally and physically upon entering school at six years. Kindergarten work done by these.

The atmosphere of the classroom was most agreeable—plain and clean, equipped with tables and chairs. Each child has his own shelf-room and coat-hook, designated by a tiny placard, with an object painted on it, e.g. a bear, a fish, etc.

The children have a lunch at 10:30, for which they bring a sandwich from home, and the school furnished milk. The children *putzen* for themselves—wash up and keep the utensils clean. They are remarkably self-restrained for six-year olds. In eating, none touched either his food or his milk, although both stood before them, until a signal was given.

Berlin, March 5, 1928

Visited the Hilfschule (Dunnkerstrasse 64). Saw the spacious provisions for the feeble-minded. This school was co-educational.

Twelve children to a class.

1. The lowest grade of children, who do not try to read, do handwork with needle and basketry mostly.

2. The higher grade of older children sewing, doing machine sewing on a Singer machine, doing woodwork by measure, bookbinding and knitting. Maps made in sand boxes. Color utilized everywhere.

Children are given two years trial in the regular schools (see account of school kindergarten, March 3). If not progressed by end of school year, placed in Hilfschule. Parents may provide private instruction if they like, but must accede to school's decision if child remains in public school.

Berlin, March 5, 1928

Visited the school for the hard of hearing (Pappelallee 40–41, Rektor Reinfeder). Saw the instruction of the pupils in lip reading and pronunciation. They repeated stories, asked each other questions, and told stories based on their Wanderung recently.

Saw demonstration of an apparatus for magnifying sound, in which the teacher spoke into a funnel-shaped megaphone, to which were attached rubber tubes with stethoscopic endings (for the ears). There was thus accommodation for twelve children. They repeated separately and in chorus what the teacher said, and their mishearings were corrected. School co-educational.

So far as the education of the backward and the handicapped was concerned, no particular new insights appeared to come from these visits to the schools of Europe. But the topic of the education of the gifted was seen in a new light, and this matter was the subject of frequent conversation and inquiry. The problem of the identification and education of the bright appeared to be peculiarly an American phenomenon. In the machinery of the British and the continental schools of that day there was no urge applied to every child to pursue the educational system to its very peak. Duller and average minds were automatically eliminated when they reached their presumably proper level. Scholarships in some abundance were available so that the bright children, even of the poor, could make a competitive showing and thus be assisted to more advanced training. To some extent at least the educational system was itself a vast device for identifying the able and encouraging the dull or average to guide their ambitions in terms of their endowment.

The American system, on the other hand, seemed almost to be geared in reverse, doing its best to conceal the existence of the able. Since every child was urged to hope to "become President," all pupils were by law detained in school, often until adulthood, or so long as the tolerance of teachers would permit. More or less mechanically they moved along from grade to grade, into high school and out to college. Meanwhile the really gifted pupils, fewer in number, were forced to mark time. They, rather than the dull, became the "laggards" and the "retarded," because the accomplishments expected of them and permitted to them were so woefully below the achievements of which they were easily capable. If nothing but this observation had come from the educational inspections abroad, the trouble involved in these school tours would have been worth while.

22

At Public School 500 (Speyer School)

The founding of Public School 500 marked a new departure in the history of educational experimentation in the New York City schools. In 1934 a Committee on Individualization had been set up by the Board of Superintendents, and the adaptation of the school to the needs and capacities of the individual was being emphasized more vigorously than ever. At about the same time the Advanced School of Education was organized at Teachers College to favor the development of research and the training of advanced professional workers. Coincidentally the Speyer School building belonging to the College, with a history of many experimental uses, became available for some new projects.

Through cooperative effort Public School 500 was established by the Board of Education, in the Speyer building provided by Teachers College. The object of the new experimental school was to investigate the education of special groups of pupils. These were: (1) slow learners (Binet Classes) with Intelligence Quotients ranging from 75 to 90, and constituting a large proportion of the public school population in the elementary grades of the metropolitan area; and (2) rapid learners (Terman Classes) with Intelligence Quotients ranging upward from 130 as high as they might be found, constituting a very small but unappreciated number of pupils. The actual range of this group at the time of the first report was from 130 to 194 I.Q.

The City was to provide the teachers and the standard elementary school equipment. The College was to assign specialists to guide the experimental studies to devise curricula, to advise concerning methods, and to conduct researches into the problems for the investigation of which the school was founded.

Although still deluged with the data, interviews and follow-up enterprises dating from the P. S. 165 project of fourteen years earlier, Leta S. Hollingworth entered with her usual enthusiasm into this program on the condition that the problems of the gifted child be included and two classes for them established. She was designated Educational Adviser for the classes for these children. The project was established by express agreement for a period of five years, beginning February, 1936.

In an address to the Faculty and Trustees on "What is Going On at Speyer School?" among other details was included a very informal account of the circumstances attending the founding of the school, and a few extracts from that address will throw some light on this history.

> I happened to meet Dr. Mort in the staff lunch room.... He said to me "Where are you going to sit?" I said, "Here." He said "Well I will sit here too, and we'll have a talk about Speyer School."
>
> Now it would be easy, it would be *edifying*, it is indeed *tempting*, for me to say that I welcomed most heartily the idea ... that Speyer School should become a school for *exceptional children*; that arrangements were forthwith concluded between the Board of Education and the College for such a school; and that this worthy venture was immediately brought to pass out of a clear sky, amidst the rejoicings of all concerned.
>
> However, such was *not* the case. The fact is that I was by no means overjoyed at the trend this conversation was taking.... For truth to tell ... my frame of reference at the moment was all set for spending the rest of my days in *restful* research with *adults*. I shall explain how I came to be in this frame of reference.
>
> Years ago, back in 1916, then young and full of notions, I should have *loved* to hear of Speyer School being vacant. I *wanted* badly to start a school for exceptional children there, but fate decreed otherwise. So in 1922 I went to the school of Mr. Jacob Theobald, Public School 165, Manhattan, and there we started classes for children above 135 I.Q. (Stanford-Binet), eight and nine year olds; and we wrought with diligence upon the whole child for three brief years; and then we watched them through high school, and then fascinated with what we saw, we watched them through college; and just as Dr. Mort began to speak to me these 56 youngsters were out of college, and I was fixing to observe them, and *them only*, for *the rest of my life*.
>
> ... Well, having gone through everything one goes through with in the course of first-hand, direct study of 56 children, from 1922 to 1935, my climate of opinion was such that all my plans were laid

to go right on for years with 56 charming *adults,* who would show no further phases of child and adolescent behavior. Can you *blame* me? . . .

(But there was) an emergent issue here that did not wither in the climate of opinion. The education of exceptional children is *not* just another one of "those things." It is an issue solidly based on the verifiable facts of educational psychology. . . .

On January 28, 1936, the Board of Education passed a resolution creating Speyer School a laboratory school for the study of the education of exceptional children, creating at the same time a new serial number for elementary schools, P. S. 500. On February 3, 1936, we opened the school.

After this account of the very beginning of the project, and a vividly illustrated story of the sort of problem encountered in the endeavors of the bright pupil to adjust to the routine school machine and to current social attitudes, she gave in this address the following very brief statement of the activities of the school.

What now is going on at Speyer School, instead of learning to read upside down, getting writer's cramp from writing innumerable digits, or carrying dusty books from cellar to garret? How shall we educate these rapid learners, who will be the most intelligent citizens of their generation? It is much too large a subject to be discussed briefly.

We are teaching them the prescribed subject matter of the elementary school curriculum, which takes about half of their time. In addition, we are helping them to learn *The Evolution of Common Things* in approximately fifteen fundamental areas of civilized human life. Also we are giving them one foreign language . . . a study of food from the standpoint of nutrition . . . instruction in swimming . . . I only wish I had time to tell you all. . . .

. . . I can't even speak of our observations on *emotional education,* the special problems of general conduct which arise for the *very gifted child,* and for him *only,* as a function of his *great* degree of deviation from the mass of his contemporaries.

"Bright children can take care of themselves?" How can they, under the compulsory education laws? Under the child labor law? Under restraint of all established sorts? This sentiment is a piece of the prevailing attitude of American philanthropy, politics and education, where concern is for the mediocre, or more especially for the incompetent; which would give all to the *burdens* of society, and little or nothing to the *burden-bearers*. Is there in America a kind of unfortunate malice toward the superior person?

In citing these remarks in brief summary we have anticipated much that might be said in greater detail about the work of Speyer School and its classes for the bright. The difficulties involved in the organization and conduct of such an enterprise had all to be lived through again. Once more the task of surveying the elementary schools of the boroughs began, in the endeavor to find 50 children of the proper age (7–9 years), of the requisite intelligence, able to travel the necessary distances, and agreeable to transfer. One of the most strenuous tasks was that of keeping the racial and national origins proportionate to the ratios found in the general school population of the city. The P. S. 165 children were predominantly from one census group, and it was desired to make the new classes more fully representative. Only by the stern diligence of the Adviser was this distribution of familial and cultural backgrounds achieved.

The chief impediment in the enterprise was that although experiments were to be undertaken, no personnel and no resources were provided for such activity. Taking the classes for rapid learners as her province, Leta S. Hollingworth inspired many volunteer helpers to undertake the researches. The resources she provided from her summer session earnings. She invited parents and friends to contribute bits of needed furniture, tools, books and materials not in the standard lists. Necessities, evaded by both of the founding institutions, such as partitions, seating changes, plumbing repairs, library shelves, she managed to have done by well-wishers with a mechanical bent but no union card.

Teachers of the special classes contributed many items that were needed and could not be officially secured. Graduate students were enlisted in research and special teaching experiments. Several advanced students with professional interests in the field gave unbelievable amounts of time and energy in their devotion to the aims and work of the experiment. From the private funds made available, the personal needs of many of the pupils were met. Some interest was shown by other professors in the College, and all were encouraged to make the best possible use of the school, under a code of ethical procedure that Leta S. Hollingworth had been driven to formulate by her earlier experience.

Public School 500, in the old Speyer building, speedily became known and often referred to as "Leta Hollingworth's school for bright children," although seven of the nine classes contained slow learners only, and it was the interest in these that had first led to the establishment of the experimental school. Unprecedented public interest was manifested and one of the heavy duties soon became handling the reporters, the feature writers, photographers, and visitors, who arrived in what seemed like a steady stream.

Some of the children of the school, without benefit of any clipping bureau, made a scrapbook of articles and editorials about the school that came to their attention up to September, 1939. Examination of this scrapbook shows the following very incomplete tabulation of such accounts:

Newspaper or Magazine	Number of Articles
New York Times	16
New York Sun	6
World Telegram (N.Y.)	4
Herald Tribune (N.Y.)	3
N. Y. Post	1

There were articles from papers in San Francisco, Philadelphia, Peekskill, and The Hague; articles from *Teachers College News, Manhattan Teacher, The Afro-American, This Week, Literary Digest, Reader's Digest, Better Schools, West Virginia Journal of Education, Parents Magazine, Time, Report of the President of the Carnegie Corporation, Home and Food, The French Review, Western Journal of Education, Teachers College Record, Columbia University Spectator,* and six unidentified newspapers and magazine articles.

An avalanche of letters arrived—inquiries, requests, comments—so that it became wholly impossible to file them, let alone reply. Hundreds of petitions for admission, guidance, materials, or examination came in, that could not be acted on. Visitors arrived in such numbers that a guard had to be authorized to refuse admittance except on special visitors' days.

As the article in a newspaper in The Hague shows, interest reached foreign shores. Letters in various languages arrived, and visitors and inspectors from foreign lands. Addressing the graduating class at the school in the spring of 1939, Leta S. Hollingworth told them:

> The units of work which our pupils and teachers have formulated and published have been called for all over the City, all over the United States, and all over the world.

At Public School 500 (Speyer School)

I have sent at request samples of the units formulated . . . to far places, like South Africa; Beirut, Syria; Saskatchewan, Canada; Melbourne, Australia; Sofia, Bulgaria; London, England. . . . An educator from New York City recently sailed for an international conference on education in Geneva, Switzerland. He took with him 25 copies of the various units of work from this school. . . .

The "units" referred to in the foregoing quotation were sections of one of the enrichment projects which Leta S. Hollingworth was particularly interested in seeing developed. The curricular problem for bright children was far from settled, and, as she put it, "there is no body of revealed wisdom about this matter." But she recognized the futility of giving such children mathematics and languages and other abstract material merely as "discipline," and there was no point in introducing them in advance to subjects they would later meet in high school and college. She had observed the inexpedience of simple rapid promotion, for this brought bright children to the advanced grades while still too small and too immature emotionally and socially to make good adaptations with others so much older. Her conclusions were expressed in the following words:

> Turning to more positive considerations, we know that these pupils—they and no others—will possess as adults those mental powers on which the learned professions depend for conservation and advancement . . . they will be the literary interpreters . . . of their generation; . . . the ones who can think deeply and clearly about abstractions like the state, the government and economics. . . . As for *originations, . . . only a few can produce them in the realm of abstractions. . . . The education of the best thinkers should be . . . for initiative and originality. Effective originality depends first of all upon sound and exhaustive knowledge of what the course of preceding events has been. . . . The intellectually gifted need especially to know what the evolution of culture has been . . . at eight or nine years what they need to know is the evolution of culture as it has affected common things.*

On this basis areas of study were mapped out, such as food, shelter, clothing, transportation, sanitation and health, trade, time-keeping, illumination, tools and implements, communication, law, government, education, warfare, punishment, labor, recreation. This plan was deliberately formulated, with psychological insight, as shown in the following statements:

> Between the ages of seven and thirteen years the minds of these children are occupied primarily with exploration of the world.... They are full of questions of fact, not yet being distracted by the emotional and dynamic interests that come with adolescence and adulthood. This is the golden age of the intellect. Why? How? When? Who? Where? What? are constantly on their tongues....
>
> Every one of these areas of human culture affords the opportunity and necessity for studying the evolution of common things, satisfying the intellectual curiosity, and challenging the power of learning of the children here considered.

And so *The Evolution of Common Things* became the core of the enrichment curriculum. As the groups worked out these projects with the guidance and encouragement of the teachers, the materials they discovered and organized were brought together by the teachers into "work units." Activities in other school work could also be effectively tied to and animated by these projects. As each unit was completed the material was published by the Board of Education in a separate pamphlet or "Curriculum Bulletin." It was these Bulletins, intended simply to show the kind of things such children could do themselves when merely guided by the teachers, that were in such demand. The editions were speedily exhausted.

By November, 1939, such bulletins had been issued on Aviation, Communication, Transportation by Land, Illumination, Shelter, A unit on Time and Timekeeping, not yet published, was specially filmed in color and shown periodically at the World's Fair in New York City by agents of the Board of Education.

There were other enrichment activities, and for some of these (French, Nutrition) bulletins also appeared. A similar series of bulletins appeared from the slow-learner classes, on such topics as We Visit the Orient, Public Services and Utilities, Our City, Biography.

New features introduced into the study of the activities in this third educational experiment by Leta S. Hollingworth took the form of many photographs and motion picture films of the children at work, and of the products of this work. The public press, then strongly picture conscious, made much use of such materials, and the films contributed interest and enthusiasm on the expeditions afield to "carry the message to Garcia." Leta S. Hollingworth was not content to rely on such professional photographs and films as were occasionally made possible. Provided with Kodak and motion picture camera she took with her own hands and also edited and titled hundreds of photographs and thousands of feet of 8 mm. film. When set-ups and lighting were arranged for the World's Fair film, and the photographers followed the children on their trips, taking standard commercial films, she was always on hand with her own instrument. Thus she secured, for what she called her "modern lecture notes," her own films for the whole unit. Many other films were taken by her of pupils, activities, and school products.

When her work was interrupted she had, in connection with the school, many projects under way that are not likely to be completed by other hands. There was to be a book tentatively entitled "Teaching the Tops," half text and half pictures. There was planned a collection and reprinting of all the Curriculum Bulletins. A series of lantern slides was under way, to supplement the films as instructional material. Projects on poetry, on biography, and on argumentation had been started, as well as further units in *The Evolution of Common Things*. Several special researches had also been outlined and some of these may be carried to completion by other interested workers who were associated with her in the P. S. 500 experiments.

On the wall in the main entrance to Speyer School is a beautiful plaque, bearing the striking profile of Leta S. Hollingworth, with the inscription:

> IN LOVING AND GRATEFUL MEMORY OF OUR DEVOTED FRIEND
> DR. LETA S. HOLLINGWORTH
> THE CHILDREN OF SPEYER SCHOOL, P.S. NO. 500, 1939

The Board of Superintendents, of the City of New York, who had established P. S. 500 in conjunction with Teachers College, on December 12, 1939, adopted "a resolution of tribute to Leta S. Hollingworth." Among other things this resolution included the following paragraphs:

> For the last two decades Dr. Hollingworth has voluntarily served as guide and counsellor in research efforts concerned with the education of exceptional pupils in our schools. Convinced that a teachers college in our city can best develop its teacher training program by articulating closely with the public schools of the city, Dr. Hollingworth was always ready to cooperate with our supervisors.
> Her able leadership in the study of exceptional children has been an inspiration to administrators and teachers not only in New York but in other cities.
> Dr. Hollingworth's guidance in the experiment with intellectually gifted children served to emphasize the importance of further studies of the needs of rapid learners. Her personal interest in each member of the two

classes for intellectually gifted children assisted in discovering the talents and capacities of each child, and in developing instructional materials and techniques which would help them achieve their fullest growth.

We believe that the schools have suffered a serious loss by the removal of a leader of the exceptional vision and devotion to duty that characterized Dr. Hollingworth's educational career.

Of the various formal honors received by Leta S. Hollingworth during her lifetime the one that she cherished most was the honorary degree of L.L.D. conferred on her by her Alma Mater, the University of Nebraska. At the Commencement at which this degree was conferred, she also had occasion to introduce to the people of her native state her favorite theme—the importance of gifted minds.

23

A Doctor of Laws

In the spring of 1938 Leta S. Hollingworth was unofficially told an academic secret by her life-long friend, Professor Louise Pound, one of her favorite professors at the University of Nebraska and still on that faculty. This was that she should accept no engagements for the Commencement period that year, so as to be free to come to Lincoln, Nebraska, at that time if it should seem desirable. In due time official letters came from the Chancellor of the University of Nebraska, informing her that at the 67th Commencement, on Monday, June 6th of that year, her presence would be welcomed. The Faculty, Senate, and Regents of her Alma Mater wished on that occasion to confer on her the honorary degree of Doctor of Laws.

Just thirty-two years had gone by since the day in June, 1906, when she had read the class poem, received her Bachelor's degree and her Phi Beta Kappa key at that institution. During those years she had become a national leader in the field of education. Her books were in use on the campus where she had enrolled for her first course of study in that field. She had previously been invited to come there for a summer session engagement, but had been already committed to another obligation and could not go.

Several members of the faculty whom she had known as a student were still on active duty. There were many friendships dating from college years that could be renewed. There would be an opportunity to revisit old scenes and to revive fading memories. Her husband was to receive, along with her at this Commencement, the same honorary degree. Together they could explore the campus, the city, and the countryside, much as they had done so often in their junior and senior years, as classmates who had agreed to meet life side by side.

There was indeed a special touch of sentiment in coming back together to the old campus, to stand side by side in the grand new auditorium and receive from the people of their native state an unsought symbol of appreciation of their work. The early years of struggle and uncertainty on that campus were not forgotten. It would be a joy to take again the same walks, to sit under the same trees, free from doubt and anxiety, and with the memories of a third of a century of contented life and work together. And so they returned to Nebraska that spring and attended Commencement in the University Coliseum. It had been built on almost the very spot where in the spring of 1905 Leta Stetter and her classmate had agreed to take up life's challenge together.

After the Commencement ceremonies were over, an Alumni Luncheon was to take place. This annual event was attended by many notables of the state, as well as by distinguished alumni, the recipients of honorary degrees, and officers of the University. Leta S. Hollingworth was asked to give the address at this banquet. She was in high spirits and before her address she had engaged the Governor of the state, alongside whom she sat, in lively conversation about Nebraska as it had been and then was.

For her address she had chosen a topic that neatly combined her active interest in the gifted with her enthusiasm for her native state. This topic was "The Participation of Nebraska in the Intellectual and Artistic Leadership of the Nation." She began by referring to her early days in the state, and her later life away from it:

> Time and distance teach one many things about Nebraska. Of all that I have learned I can formulate but a small part here. I shall speak only of how Nebraska spreads through the intellectual and artistic life of our nation, and influences the thought and conduct of America in ways which can be but vaguely guessed without actual study of the matter.

She then cited the available statistical data showing the place of the various states of the union in the production of American men and women of distinction. She showed that, according to studies made by other individuals not especially interested in that state, "Nebraska was found to rank *third* among the states in the production of American notables of the nineteen-twenties, being bettered by Massachusetts and Connecticut only."

Two other studies, particularly of the production of men and women of science, were quoted. Here also the place of Nebraska was unexpectedly high, in spite of its relative youth.

The Nebraskans thus participating in the mental life of the nation were born on the average 45 years earlier than the decade of their notability.... Therefore they came into being under pioneering conditions. Do the rigors of pioneering teach habits of hard work? Or was there something in the breed of the people who first settled the plains of Nebraska that was exceptional? Was the result perhaps a joint outcome of *both* of these conditions?

Is Nebraska today producing the American notables of the future in the same ratio as it produced those of the nineteen-twenties? No one knows. Have pioneering conditions disappeared? Has the human stock changed in kind or quality? Who can say?

This address was of course heard with rare attention and enthusiasm by the Alumni of the University and the representatives of the state. One thought at once of the pioneer origin and the pioneer life of the speaker. Only a few months later the American Educational Research Association, assembled at St. Louis, was to pass a resolution of tribute to that speaker, in the course of which it was said:

> Professor Hollingworth's whole life was spent in pioneering. In a "homecoming" letter printed in the *Nebraska State Journal* a year before her death she stated—"I was part of the frontier.... As a child I saw my grandfather's plow turn miles of prairie that had never been cut before.... All my memories are of the 'sod house frontier,' where I acquired a splendid set of work habits and all the benefits to be derived from mastering farm animals, blizzards, sand storms and cacti."
>
> During her professional career she was no less the pioneer, and had no less need for ability to withstand new types of blizzards, storms and cacti.

At the request of the university authorities she wrote out the words of this stirring address. It was widely printed in the papers of Nebraska, and the University published it as a special Bulletin under its own seal, for general distribution. Some of the reason for this enthusiasm, and some of the quality of thought and utterance characteristic of Leta S. Hollingworth as a public speaker, are suggested by the closing paragraph of the address:

> In its early days Nebraska produced many more intellectual persons per million of the population than the state could itself use. So it exported the surplus for the use of the nation as a whole. Just as it exported its corn, so it exported its youths.
>
> When the state thinks of its crops, let it think of its gifted children, one of its main products. The sower that tops the Capitol sows not only corn for the United States, but he sows also *ideas* into the intellectual life of America, everywhere, through Nebraskans scattered over the nation.

24

Interests of Leta Stetter Hollingworth

The hierarchy of interests of a professional teacher are easily obscured by the requirements of subject matter and the specialization of research that modern investigation involves. Yet this hierarchy of interests is in some ways the major aspect of a personality. How shall it be portrayed? A somewhat clinical procedure would be to have one who was long and intimately acquainted render a subjective picture of the person he knew. A more objective method would be to have a group of less intimate acquaintances, yet close friends, give some sort of consensus of opinion or ranking of traits or interests. There would be discrepancies between the two methods, and yet no doubt a good deal of agreement, and even some truth in the discrepancies.

In the present instance I have chosen instead a third and still more objective method of trying to show, however poorly, some of the personal characteristics of a versatile individual. These characteristics should be easily recognized by her friends, but they are in part masked, in daily life, by the restrictions and limitations of professional behavior.

If the interests of an individual in this or that topic reveal that individual's deeper lying and more fundamental traits, what is needed is some objective indication of the frequency with which these interests are given expression incidentally, with no deliberate intent of disclosing their relative strength. If every time a reader saw an interesting item in a newspaper he should clip it out and preserve it, a study of these clippings might in a more than superficial way reveal the range and hierarchy of that reader's interests. Even if all topics are not equally represented in a given issue, sooner or later nearly every topic gets into the papers.

Interests of Leta Stetter Hollingworth

Leta S. Hollingworth was an eager collector of clippings. Scarcely a newspaper but left her hand mutilated, the clippings to be hastily stored away until some convenient time when they might be appropriately inserted in memoranda or notes. A pile of 215 such clippings had accumulated on and in her desk, and examination of them rather faithfully reflects the hierarchy of her casual interests and their variety. According to their content, this pile of clippings yields the following classification:

Nebraska, The Frontier (7 each)	14
Difficulties and adjustments of the young	14
Social and economic problems	13
Poems	12
Jokes and cartoons	10
Achievements by women	9
Jews	9
Music	9
Books	9
Distinguished men she admired	9
Chess, Bridge (4 each)	8
Schools and education	8
Evolution of common things	7
Fakes, fraud, magic	6
Bridges	5
Horses	5
Genius and fame	5
Housing and clothing	4
Prodigies (children)	4
Quotations	4
Freaks and oddities	4
Honors and awards	3
Cowboys and cattle	3
Theatre and ballet	3
Peculiarities of words	3
Psychology and psychiatry	3
Eating places in New York	3
Recipes	3
Photography	3
Sports	3

Travel, Current Events, Ethics, Biography, Sales and auctions, Marriage and weddings	2 each
Movies, Friends, Aluminum, China, Woodwork, Medicine, Investments, Radio, Birds	1 each

We need not assume that all one's values appear in a collection of clippings. Perhaps our most abiding and most precious values are least likely to appear there. But these would relate to highly personal themes and people, and to relationships which it is not our purpose to inquire into here. The topics in such a list of clippings more nearly portray the attractiveness of transient things presented by the environment at large, not those closely involved in the privacy of self and home. We are here inquiring not into the affections but merely into interests.

In this list even the least frequent items occur for some reason, and betray a real interest, for each clipping represents a genuine act. *Movies* and *Radio* attracted her because of their educational possibilities. She believed that skill in both should be acquired by teachers. She talked over the networks whenever opportunity offered "to get practice"; and she had just completed the taking, editing, and titling of 2,000 feet of 8 mm. motion picture film of enrichment activities at Speyer School for what she called her "modern lecture notes."

Aluminum, Woodwork, China, as well as leather, glass, precious stones and all the materials shaped by the handcraftsman were among physical objects she most enjoyed. A leather wallet, a well-woven quirt, a good piece of binding or luggage could afford her exquisite pleasure. She was herself an excellent seamstress and in early years her dresses, tailored suits, coats, and hats, as well as some of her husband's shirts, were made at home.

Friends were her most cherished possessions, and any mention of them in the papers was always clipped. To *Investments* she was not wholly indifferent and she managed her own broker's account with more than average astuteness. She continued to be actively interested in *Medicine* after her professional experience as a clinical psychologist in Bellevue Hospital and at the Post-Graduate Medical School. All these interests were lively ones, even though represented in each case by but a single clipping in this last small collection.

That she was awake to *Current Events,* enjoyed *Travel,* was addicted to *Auctions* and often attended them, the clippings reveal. All these come in for two mentions. Nor did she ever cease to be interested in *Marriage* as an institution. Her enthusiasm for *Biography* is shown also by her repeated use of it as an enrichment project in teaching bright children. As for *Ethics,* also in this group, our earliest sober discussion was on the topic "Should the strong bear the infirmities of the weak?" In fact this issue was discussed for thirty-four years without a final decision. In later years she was much concerned over how the young, lacking a religious creed, could arrive at principles of conduct for their own lives.

If frequency is a criterion, *Cowboys and Cattle, Sports, Eating Places, Recipes,* the *Theatre and Ballet,* were still more active interests. In all these her pleasure was keen. She would at any opportunity attend a horse show, an ice carnival, the circus, the serious theatre, a new restaurant. She went to the races and also a prize fight, to see if she might like them, but was disappointed in both. She was an ardent tennis player in her younger days, and she often went to the Forest Hills tournaments, preferably taking a party of friends. *Games, Sports,* and all *competitive* activities were a very special interest, and she never wholly satisfied her appetite for them.

Eating Places intrigued her and in the search for good ones she sampled many. A major complaint was that next time she tried to find them they had so often disappeared. She was a skilled cook herself, although in general she did not like housework, in all aspects of which she had had long experience. The items *Psychology* and *Psychiatry* reflect a professional complex, but *Words* and *Photography* were two of her major hobbies.

As a small child she kept scrapbooks of *Actresses,* filled memorandum books with choice *Quotations,* and rode *Horses* at every opportunity. Even the solemn warning that horseback riding was both atavistic and dangerous in our day did not deter her. Among her most recent acquisitions were a rawhide quirt and a can of saddle soap. She early learned *Household* duties and the care and manufacture of *Clothing.* All these items are represented in the clippings with more than median frequency.

That *Bridges* should stand so high, along with *Prodigies, Genius,* and *Oddities,* there is no explanation for. But every one of the items in this list with four or five clippings I recognize as tied to strong interests, actively present since I first knew her at the age of eighteen.

She played *Chess* and *Bridge* with zest, and these two competitive games stand in the list along with *Evolution of Common Things,* which was a fairly recent but strong interest, connected with the enrichment program for gifted children. That *Schools* and *Education* should rank so close to *Fakes, Fraud,* and *Magic* may appear sinister in a Teachers College professor. Yet, once you get over the first shock, they do not sit badly together.

The items thus far up the list may appear to represent casual or at most professional interests. But the ten topics that head the list are represented by so many clippings that something more fundamental might be tapped by them. This I know to be the case.

Achievement of any sort she thoroughly enjoyed, and the joy was enhanced if the achievement were accomplished by a woman. She had for years been preoccupied with "woman's dilemma," the conflict between professional endeavor and reproductive function. She had long been collecting, as has already been recorded, material for a projected volume to be called "Mrs. Pilgrim's Progress." Those who know her scientific work will recognize this as the field of her earliest researches.

But, with characteristic impartiality and justice, *Distinguished Men* as an item has precisely the same number of clippings. There was a long list of men whose character or activities she found particularly interesting. As random examples might be cited Andrew Carnegie, Abraham Lincoln, Nicholas Murray Butler, Cordell Hull, Roscoe Pound, Huey Long, Francis Galton, Lewis M. Terman.

Although not musically trained, she loved *Music* for its own sake, and she systematically tried to cultivate knowledge and appreciation of it. She preferred instrumental music to the human voice; string quartettes and chamber music were her favorites, but she also had a special interest in Indian and Hawaiian melodies.

That *Jews* should be represented by as many clippings as *Books* is no surprise to those who knew her well. *Books* were in a sense her major interest, but since her residence in New York *Jews* and issues connected with them would often displace *Books* in her conversation. Perhaps this topic belongs higher up the list under the heading *Social Problems.*

Still more characteristic, and closely related to some of the topics just considered, are the five items that head the frequency list. She was at heart merry and playful. She loved *Jokes* and *Stories* if they were good, and *Cartoons* if they were apt. Not only did she clip such items with avidity, she also put them to good use in enlivening her lectures and addresses. Her own sense of humor was alert and ready, and she was able to laugh her way through many a minor calamity.

In later years few but her intimates knew of her keen and perennial interest in *Poetry.* The writing of poems and stories was an occupation she always enjoyed when she had time for it and much of her leisure, which was scant, was passed in reading the poets. A collection of her own poems, found among her papers, has just been printed, and there is also a group of stories. As an undergraduate, as has already been told, she majored in English and from her sophomore year on she was a reader in the English Department, to which two of her favorite professors belonged. She had a fine feeling for *Words*—their usage, their sound, their spelling, their derivation and relations, and a strong passion for accuracy and precision in the use of language. Her own style in speech and in writing possessed all of the classical virtues, besides being animated, direct, and convincing.

That *Social Problems,* and especially difficulties encountered by *Youth* were among her major concerns, her own writings testify. One of her most influential volumes was *The Psychology of the Adolescent.* Several of the items lower in the list might also have been included here to swell the totals. This interest was not in speculations and abstractions. It was first of all in concrete, personal, social and educational predicaments and their practical solution. I have already estimated that she gave personal psychological counsel to at least 4,000 individuals during her years of work at Teachers College.

She was often impatient with those who assured her that time and progress would solve many *Social Problems,* and she was strong for immediate action. She marched in suffrage parades, served as watcher at the polls, appeared in person before authorities, boards, legislatures and commissions, always with telling facts at her command, constructive suggestions, and intrepid defence of her program. These statements should not convey a false impression. She was far from being a busybody; she preferred a life of reflection and scholarship; but she did not hesitate to register her beliefs when the time seemed to call for that. She deplored minor executive politics and her detestation of any appearance of self-seeking often handicapped her in the promotion of causes in which she might seem to be personally involved.

Along with these topics, in her hierarchy of interests, stands her native state, *Nebraska,* and the western *Frontier.* This interest is strongly biographical. Her ancestors were all pioneers, who played their own part in the "winning of the West." She was herself the first white child born in Dawes County, Nebraska. She was born in a dugout, reared in a log cabin, and first attended school in a log schoolhouse. Her earliest memories, as she has recorded, were of cowboys, longhorn cattle, Indians, army posts, round-ups, pack-wagons, blizzards, dust storms, sandhills, ponies, and the building of the Northwestern Railroad.

In this environment she began, before she was sixteen, to write poems for the local papers, to send manuscripts to *McClure's* and other magazines, to collect quotations from almanacs and chance books, to play with words and phrases, and to assemble pictures and accounts of men and women of achievement.

Little wonder that *Frontier Life* and *Difficulties of Youth* stood at the top in the hierarchy of her later clippings; that *Prairie Years* was chosen as the title for the incomplete collection of poems from her hand; that when asked by an editor in her native state to write a "home-coming" letter for his paper, she did so with enthusiasm. The closing paragraph of this letter, which was quoted on an earlier page, reflects clearly the profound affection she had for the region and the people of her childhood.

It may be added to this story of her clippings that her consuming interest in her later years does not appear clearly in the list. Items relating to it were probably not casually stored away, but immediately incorporated in lectures, writings, and addresses. This dominant interest was in the highly intellectual young who are handicapped, perhaps by not being understood, perhaps by poverty. There is little doubt that this interest also was biographically derived, at least in part.

Among a group of "rapid-learners" Leta S. Hollingworth would certainly have been one of the speediest. Until she reached college she also must have been misunderstood, unappreciated, and mistreated; she also knew poverty, not only in her childhood but also in her later years. She paid her own way through college after her Freshman year, by long hours of theme reading. She then supported herself and gave aid to others, by high-school teaching. This she abandoned to become the wife of an instructor with a salary of $1,000 in New York City. Against this handicap she struggled to achieve her own professional training, to pay her fees, make her own clothes, print her dissertation, and to help sick relatives. She very well knew the fallacies underlying the slogan, "The bright can take care of themselves."

Out of this personal experience certainly in part grew her profound and permanent interest in bright children, and her scorn for that quaint conception of "philanthropy" that directs its benefits "toward the burdens of society, rather than toward the burden bearers."

Her own character and abilities ultimately brought her, at what cost we do not know, to circumstances in which she could freely indulge her own hierarchy of interests with reasonable security. To those she left behind it is a mitigating comfort to know that in her last few years she could place the fruits of her effort in ways she hoped might bring the greatest good through the more welcome recognition and the fostering of such natural resources as she herself so well symbolized.

25

Personal and Home Life

Leta S. Hollingworth was best known to the world at large as a scholar and an educator, and it is mainly in these respects that this account of her life has tried to describe her. To those who knew her more intimately she was the rarest of personalities and a precious friend. It is outside the present writer's ability to describe the variety of her charm and the versatility of her endowment, even if the mood were upon him to do so. A few comments about her attitudes and a little information concerning her last days represent all that this section shall undertake to give.

She was strongly social in her own inclinations, and loved to have her friends with her. She was ready with material aid whenever a friend was in trouble and a long list of generous acts could be enumerated, did this not infringe on personal relations. The ethics of personal relations meant much to her and in her dealings, not only with adults but especially with the children and their families involved in her educational experiments, she adhered scrupulously to such principles as seemed to her just and appreciative of human feelings.

She was a chief source of economic assistance to a large number of young people whose future she thought might be given high social value. Even when the outcome was disappointing, her main concern was with the nature of the factors responsible for such an outcome. She was the chief support of an array of helpless persons for whom, on one ground or another, she had an affection. But she was not a random donator and she repudiated the play of mere personal sentiment in these benefactions. In her own way she was as prodigal of her time and energy and resources as some of her ancestors had been, but her prodigality, even when miscalculated, was directed always by what she conceived to be social goals.

In the same way she would spend many days, or periods of days, taking her part in what she felt to be a worthy and new undertaking, and she collaborated easily and faithfully with others, even though she was herself convinced that cooperative projects were usually doomed to failure. Particularly in some of her addresses she stressed the importance of individual responsibility in any enterprise that was to make headway. For her, research was not hack work but creative activity, and she was as little hopeful of research to be conducted by a "committee" as she would have been of a portrait to be painted in that way, or of a sonnet written at a hastily organized "conference."

She never played into the hands of organized or professional charity, and her aid or her energy, if contributed, she tried to direct toward a burden-bearer, actual or prospective, rather than toward conventional social burdens.

She loved her own home life; it might be said to have been second only to her devotion to intellectual activity. With her husband she endured, so long as it seemed expedient, the confining life of the city and the fictitious home comfort of city apartments. But she welcomed as much as he the day when it was possible to move to the country. When this initial summer residence ultimately became a year-round practice, she was somewhat less contented with it. She had formed many associations with people and affairs in town and the life of a commuter appeared to mean breaking with some of these, although none of them were easy to abandon.

A resolute independence was one of her outstanding traits. This appeared in the conduct of her own life, in her advocacy of a revised social status for women, in her professional activities and affiliations, in her educational principles and scientific studies. She resented being helped onto a street car by polite conductors who reserved such solicitude for those of her sex. Late one night fire engines gathered in the neighborhood after people had retired. Her husband dressed and went out to investigate, promising to return and inform her at once if anything important was going on. When he shortly returned she was gone. Diligent search of the apartment building and roof failed to find her. When the fire trucks left and the neighborhood quieted down she promptly appeared. She had not waited to be behind others in her information and had gone to the scene of the fire. After it was under control she returned to the apartment where she was able to tell her distraught husband, still looking for her, all about the conflagration he had missed seeing.

Her own capacity for deep tenderness and staunch loyalty made her markedly appreciative of these traits in others, but she was discriminating and choice in the direction of her affections and had vigorous aversions as well as strong attachments. Particularly offensive to her was any inflated ego, a bluffer or pretender, quack or charlatan, and anyone or group that sought personal advantages by evading what she called "the rules of life." The quality of dependability was one of the things she valued in others and sternly cultivated in herself. Connected therewith is one of the indications that she fully realized the short time she had to live although she concealed this knowledge from others. For in her last years she wrote out documentary contracts with her personal assistants and with those she had undertaken to support through courses of study, specifying always that in the event of her death the obligations thus incurred by her should become a charge against her estate.

Although terrified of motor cars because keenly aware of their power and danger, she resolutely set herself to master driving and to acquire an operator's license. She never drove for pleasure and seldom took the wheel after she had secured her driver's permit. The first time she underwent a test for this was in an old vintage Hupmobile, in a driving rain, in the city of White Plains. Many a practiced driver would have avoided a trip in such a downpour. But the hour had been set, the examiner was on hand, and the test proceeded, without success. Later she appeared again for try-out in a new and flexible car, in decent weather, and passed the test. Her alleged reason for learning to drive was that she would be an old fogey not to be able to, and that she must be able to take her husband to the hospital some day when he might meet with an accident in his venturesome play with axes, sledges, trees, and rocks. She drove always with fear, perspiring profusely. She never did reduce the operations to an automatic level and she was not a good judge of space or distance on the road, as a safe driver must be. A severe myopia which had been characteristic of her vision all her life was in part responsible for this and without her glasses things at any distance did not appear clearly and distinctly. Perhaps this characteristic also explains in part the fact that she was always much more interested in color than in design and spatial arrangement.

Although her thinking was rigorously coherent and her writing straightforward and perfectly organized, these characteristics issued from her inner perceptions rather than from her methods of work.

When intent on a project, which was nearly always, she was oblivious to the spatial order and arrangement of her surroundings and even of her materials. She drove straight to her goal and the materials she might need she could find when they were wanted. The great amount of records, memoranda, letters, keepsakes, souvenirs, photographs, reprints, clippings, and personal equipment that she left behind her exhibited no classifications to guide strange hands that undertook to deal with them. Although it required several rooms to accommodate these things, every item seemed to have for her its psychological or chronological spot.

She apparently preserved all the letters she had received through a third of a century of active correspondence, with carbons of her replies in the case of many professional communications. All the original data from her numerous studies were kept and the original manuscripts of her publications, most of her class lectures, and many of her public addresses. A collection of poems published since her death was assembled from a great variety of places, although an outline of their titles, or of most of them, was also found somewhere.

When she began to write a volume or an article she required no preliminary blueprint or outline to guide her. She simply began to write, and things occurred to her in a sequence and pattern that required little editing when she had finished. She needed no special nook, no prescribed surroundings, no standardized equipment for her writing. Given paper, and a pencil, pen or typewriter, a board, box, desk or table, and a place to sit—and she became so absorbed in her enterprise that surroundings could scarcely distract her. A similar capacity for concentrated attention appeared in her reading.

From earliest childhood reading had been one of her keenest passions. In time the very act of reading printed matter, wherever it might be encountered, became with her a compulsion so strong that it often led her into minor predicaments. Starting to wrap up a bundle in an old newspaper she would become engrossed instead with the random columns she found in the paper. The sidewalk newsstands on New York streets definitely interfered with her walking past them. A line on an exposed paper or magazine would catch her eye and arrest her progress until she had explored the contents of the newsstand. Once she absently-mindedly took the arm of a man standing alongside her. When she finally started to leave she was surprised at the resistance he offered. It was not her husband, as she had supposed, but a large colored gentleman who had not objected to her holding his arm but did not intend to be led away by a strange woman. Her myopia often led her into similarly amusing situations. Since she could not, without her glasses, recognize people at any considerable distance, often she amiably nodded or waved at random passers-by who had looked in her direction, for fear of appearing to ignore a friend.

Much of the character and personality of Leta S. Hollingworth must now have appeared in the story of her life, the description of her activities, the excerpts from her letters, the citation of her verse, the brief summaries of her books and papers, and the analysis of the newspaper clippings. All of these things could be presented in a more or less objective way, without the biographer being called on to intrude his personal evaluations.

No attempt further than these evidences need be made to summarize the attributes of character and personality that endeared her to all who knew her, and to very many that had only heard of her. There might be given examples of the estimates and expressions of regard recorded by people scattered all over the world when they learned that they had lost her; but these were never intended to be put to such a use.

Her death came as a shock to all who knew her; even her closest intimates were wholly unwarned of such an event. Ten years before, she had voluntarily sought a thorough physical examination, and had been informed of a foreign growth of which she had been unaware. She consulted the best available authorities on such conditions and reported to her family that the tumor had been declared nonmalignant in character and that she had been advised to leave it alone.

Her native health and vigor were such that the occasional mild complaints she suffered during the next ten years were not associated by her with this circumstance, or appeared not to be. They seemed in fact to be very common complaints and they received only symptomatic treatment. She steadfastly refused, however, to submit to further medical examinations, and maintained this resolute attitude even against the plea of those closest to her.

When depletion of energy and severe local complaints appeared in the fall of 1939, she explained them by overwork and arranged for a leave of absence from duty, in order to rest. Again she declined medical attention, and declared, "It would only mean a major operation." Within three weeks of the day of her death she was effectively planning to go away with a friend of long standing, who was also a nurse, "for a long rest, with no human contacts."

Only the inability of the friend to make the trip at just that time kept her from following out this plan, and only the insistent plea that it was unfair to her family for her to refuse medical investigation induced her at last to relent. Whereupon she was ordered to the hospital without delay, for surgical exploration, and little hope was extended to her family.

At the hospital the diagnosis and verdict were immediate. It was abdominal carcinoma, in an advanced stage and not operable or amenable to therapy, that was the cause of her growing weakness. In the next three weeks nothing that could be done succeeded in rallying her failing strength. On her last day, when a few more lingering weeks had been declared the best that could be hoped for, pneumonia set in and that evening she breathed her last.

No records among her papers throw any light on this baffling history. There had never been any intimation from her that she knew what was happening to her, although she was more familiar than most people with the causes of illness, and she had been closely observant of several who succumbed to the same malady as hers.

The opinion of the physicians who made her acquaintance and attended her at the hospital was that she had known from the beginning, but chose to march straight to the end and then collapse, rather than endure a life of invalidism and a series of surgical experiences destined at most only to postpone that end. Being agreed on this opinion, they expressed their amazement at the resolute courage that had maintained her in that decision through ten knowing years.

The biographer, who if anyone could, should be expected to throw light on this picture, is wholly mystified. He knew Leta S. Hollingworth longer and more closely than anyone else in the world and it is easy, now, to interpret many of her acts and plans during her later years, in the light of this explanation. But he does not surely know; he can only say that it might very well have been that way, for Leta S. Hollingworth was that kind of a woman. Even as a little child she had made a pact with life:

> That if I left out part of childhood, I should be granted other values which seemed more to be desired. Nor has life thus far failed to keep that compact.
> When I was less than ten years old I had taken a look at life and had decided that . . . some part of it must be left out. So, having a very immature conception of relative values, I decided to grow up, then and there, solemnly renouncing the rest of childhood. I sat in

an old weather-beaten sleigh and made the compact. Strangely enough, life went on in the pathway where I then set it.

What Leta S. Hollingworth was capable of doing before the age of ten, she was thoroughly capable of doing at the age of forty-three. And she was capable of sustaining this act for the remaining decade of her life.

During the last year of her life she was observed to spend more than the usual amount of her leisure moments, often in the evening, reading poetry. She was seen occasionally to mark the pages of these books, and after the last tragic day these acts were remembered, and the books examined. Some of the poems were marked with a bright red circle; their themes were love and death. Among the latter were "On a March Day," "I Have Seen the Spring," and "Beautiful, Proud Sea," from Sara Teasdale's *Dark of the Moon*; the first and fourth "Sonnets" in Part Four, and "Dirge Without Music" in Part Three, of Edna St. Vincent Millay's *The Buck in the Snow and Other Poems*.

The playing of soft music by a string quartet, which was her favorite, and the reading of these poems were the last rites for her on the occasion, when, from the little chapel in Wyuka Cemetery in Lincoln, Nebraska, she was taken by her friends to rest in the spot that she had chosen for herself, only eighteen months before.

26

The Memorial Conference

On December 13 and 14, 1940, about a year after the death of Leta S. Hollingworth, a Conference on the Education of the Gifted was held in her honor. This Conference was organized by Teachers College, Columbia University, and it convened in the halls of that institution, where for twenty-five years her presence and her work had been familiar features.

A volume entitled *Education and the Individual—In Honor of Leta S. Hollingworth,* was issued at the same time by Teachers College. This volume, the December, 1940, issue of the *Teachers College Record,* contained her complete bibliography, and summaries of her work in the six chief fields of research, written by experts in those fields, who had been her students in earlier years. The *Foreword* to this volume expresses the spirit and motive, both of the volume and of the Conference on the Gifted.

> The death of Leta S. Hollingworth, Professor of Education, on November 27, 1939, brought to an untimely close a career of great productivity and brilliance in several fields of education and psychology. After her death her friends set about formulating plans to honor and carry forward her work. They had no doubt that she herself would have restrained efforts merely to honor her but would have encouraged endeavors to enrich the fields to which she had devoted her life. It was therefore decided, as a first step, to prepare a volume designed primarily to take stock of our present status and resources, and to suggest the major future needs in these professional fields. In this issue of THE RECORD appear articles on each of the six major fields in which Professor Hollingworth taught, wrote, lectured, advised, and conducted research. Each article was written by one of her students who has done important work in the area represented and who was highly respected by her.
>
> In addition is included a bibliography of Professor Hollingworth. . . . Having in mind the same general purposes as those which led to the pub-

lication of this issue, the colleagues and friends of Professor Hollingworth have also planned a Conference on the Education of the Gifted, to be held at Teachers College on December 13–14.

The Introduction to the twelve-page program of this Conference amplifies the foregoing statement in the following words:

> This Conference on Education for the Gifted is held in honor of Leta S. Hollingworth, Professor of Education in Teachers College, whose untimely death last year brought to a close a brilliant career. Our discussions here are designed to promote increased activity in the discovery and education of the gifted—the task to which she so earnestly devoted herself and which she considered of paramount importance in our national life.
> In planning this Conference, we have felt that we might most appropriately honor Professor Hollingworth by contributing to the solution of the problems in which she was most interested....
> It is hoped that from this Conference will come plans, materials, and suggestions that will help laymen and educators to continue the work of Professor Hollingworth. This task is worthy of our best efforts; for as Professor Hollingworth has said: "Gifted minds have a positive value beyond all price."

The *Proceedings* of the Conference itself, which was participated in and attended by an array of distinguished and influential persons from many parts of the country, have been published in the January issue of the *Teachers College Record*, 1941. In the course of the addresses and discussions grateful tributes were paid to the personality and work of the woman in whose honor the Conference was organized. Extracted from their context, some of them are cited later as "expressions by others."

In addition to the addresses by the President of Columbia University, the Dean of Teachers College, and representatives of Industry, Labor, the Church, Administration, Science, and Education, various other features were impressive parts of the two-day program. A series of thirteen Seminars, with discussions by leading educators, psychologists and laymen, considered special problems connected with the education of the gifted, and their place in society. A series of Exhibits and Demonstrations of the work of classes for gifted children was presented, by cities ranging from Los Angeles to Baltimore. Demonstrations of examination and guidance techniques were given by the staff of the Guidance Laboratory, in the establishment of which Leta S. Hollingworth had played an effective role. A class of gifted children from Speyer School (P. S. 500 Manhattan), with their teacher, staged a typical class project. Motion picture films of Speyer School activities, taken by Leta S.

Hollingworth during the last few months of her life, were shown continuously in two rooms during one of the days. There were also on exhibit for the first time three volumes by or about her, these being a volume of *Public Addresses* that had just been published; the collection of verse entitled *Prairie Years*; and the volume *Education and the Individual* which had just been published in her honor.

Personal expressions of regard and sympathy contained in letters received on the occasion of her death have not been used in this story of her personality and work. There seems however to be no reason why a few of the public utterances at this Conference should not be quoted here in a final endeavor to communicate the picture of her character and influence. Some of these may be found in the *Proceedings* of the Conference on the Gifted, or were recorded in connection with plans for it. There are also included one or two spontaneous expressions by people who were in other ways motivated to give voice to their evaluations, and these will be easily identified.

> "The year's loss of friends and counsellors by death is a heavy one. It includes . . . Professor Leta S. Hollingworth, a leader in the early recognition of gifted children and in their subsequent training, who had the rare gift of combining distinguished scientific competence with the promptings of a rich and generous personality."
>
> *Report of the President, Carnegie Corporation of New York*, 1940, p. 25.

> "The death of Leta S. Hollingworth . . . brought to an untimely close a career of great productivity and brilliance in several fields of education and psychology."
>
> *Teachers College Record,* December, 1940, Vol. 42, No. 3, p. 183

> "Internationally recognized as a scientist, Professor Hollingworth realized, and in her practice demonstrated, that the application of clinical psychology is an *art*. As her friends thrilled to her spontaneity, her keen humor, and her warm sympathy, her clinical students and colleagues marvelled at her penetrating insights and her artistry."
>
> *Ibid.*, p. 202

> "Late one sultry afternoon a well-known psychologist waited patiently in the narrow corridor outside Professor Hollingworth's door while she finished testing a child.
>
> "'I came here today,' he said, 'to test against the most logical mind I know a plan for the quantitative testing of what I think is an important hypothesis. Sometimes I come to secure intensive study of a gifted child. Occasionally I come for aid in locating scientific findings on some educational problem. Often my need is aid in finding a competent person for a difficult teaching or case-work role. Most frequently however I come with

little excuse except to renew the inspiration of even a brief contact with a rare person. Always I find more than I expect in this little three-cornered office. It may be the smallest office in Teachers College, but no room is more significantly populated.'"

Ibid., p. 196

"Her work in separating these factors is summarized in a masterly article.... Her interest in feminism is perhaps epitomized in her statement that women will have to alter situations gradually so that they 'may both fulfill their intellectual promise and enjoy a normal domestic life as men have always done.'"

Ibid., p. 208

"But science is not enough, wise friend and teacher. Always there must be the person. Your service was not alone discovery, knowing, sharing; yours was the profession of Living. You had the vision to see, the courage to do, the integrity to live.... We needed Leta Hollingworth."

Ibid., p. 205

"Students and colleagues will remember her for her academic gifts and successions of students who never saw her will study her work, but I shall always remember her as a charming hostess with an amazing sense of humor."

A Letter from Edinburgh

"She was a very rare person.... She was always frank, intelligent, kindly, never evasive, and always devoted to the advancement of truth and real service to children. We shall not see her like again soon, I fear."

General Secretary, American Association for the Advancement of Science

"She was among the first to begin the systematic accumulation of facts which led to an impersonal and sound knowledge of the needs and characteristics of subnormal children.... Here, for the first time, were presented with a minimum of technical detail and a simplicity and clarity of vocabulary, the most important findings to date in the field ... as well as the practical implications of these findings for education. The basic psychological concepts, of which the book treats, have changed but little in the minds of scientists in the last two decades. It is still the best book of its kind in the field."

Teachers College Record, December, 1940, Vol. 42, No. 3, p. 231

"Her description of the adolescent period does not conform to any psychological school of thought, nor does it follow any 'authority.' It is notable for simplicity of style, methodical and well organized thinking, reliance upon objective, statistical or experimental data, common sense, freedom from popular but untenable hypotheses, and, finally, concern with the practicable and the workable."

Ibid., p. 250

"For years, long before I ever met her except through her books, I had a kind of hero-worship for her."

A Graduate Student

"By her colleagues in Education she will doubtless be remembered as an educator, but to her many friends and acquaintances in the field of psychology she was a psychologist. An examination of her researches and her numerous publications will clearly justify her title to a place among the eminent psychologists of her time.... This bare recital of scientific aims and achievements leaves untouched the record of a kindly, sympathetic, and at the same time vigorous and courageous personality."

American Journal of Psychology,
April, 1940, p. 299

"I knew Mrs. Hollingworth very well, and I consider her to have been not only an outstanding psychologist but at the same time an able, friendly and effective human being. In her death psychology has lost one who might well be called America's most distinguished woman psychologist."

*President, American Psychological Association,
on the occasion of the Memorial Conference*

"My spirit has been completely crushed by the death of Leta Hollingworth. You know how truly she was my friend.... Knowing your own friendship for her, I know you will understand how terribly upset and demoralized I feel and my certainty that we both have lost the rarest friend any person can hope to have."

*To an officer of Teachers College,
from a professor in another institution*

"The contribution of Leta S. Hollingworth ... cannot be approached through an easy separation of her achievements as original research worker, masterly teacher, and skilled case counsellor. Widely recognized as are these distinguished contributions, her greatest influence in all these activities probably arose, not from her many-sided competence, but from her fundamental integrity as a person. That influence will long continue."

Teachers College Record,
December, 1940, Vol. 42, No. 3, p. 196

"She wrote what is doubtless the most penetrating analysis ever offered of the characteristics, problems and educational needs of all types of individuals, normal and unstable, bright and dull, talented and defective, during the teens."

Science, January 5, 1940, pp. 9–11

"... she introduced a new approach and a new point of view. She broke sharply with traditional psychology which placed major emphasis upon psychological abstractions. Her plan was to use the methods of psychology and other sciences primarily for the purpose of the further understanding of human beings. No psychologist of her generation has more clearly or consistently made his work a study of 'the whole child.' During her entire professional career Professor Hollingworth's work was a brilliant example of what has been hailed, during the last ten years, as the 'new psychology, the psychological study of the individual'."

Proceedings of the American Educational Research Association, Meeting at St. Louis, Mo., February, 1940

"A charming scholar and a leader of greatest consequence and importance in this field."

From an address by the President of Columbia University

"She belongs to the group of pioneers, fated to speak the truth, whether it is acceptable to people in general or not."

N.Y. Times Book Review

"Dr. Hollingworth was always a quiet person, she didn't show how important a person she was. She was always greeting and talking to us whenever she met us. She spent hours after working at school, taking the trouble to plan things for the children. . . . Our class will always remember her as a kind and cheerful person that made Speyer School what it is today. She will live in our hearts long after we leave this school. Not only the class but the people that know her will miss her as much as I do."

Spontaneous letter from a child in Speyer School, December 13, 1939

The appropriately conceived Memorial Conference on the Education of the Gifted, in honor of the memory of Leta S. Hollingworth, was an effective and an inspiring reminder of a beautiful life, dedicated to the social good. Varied people, with diverse interests, from all parts of the nation, assembled here to commemorate her influence. Some of these knew her best in her youth, when she wrote sonnets and short stories, was college editor, class poet and university reader in English literature. They knew her best for her passion for Beauty, her felicity of verbal expression, her graceful animation and lively wit, and her exquisite sensitiveness to human relations. Others knew her first in her later years when, as a psychologist of distinction and an influential educational leader, she found her place in the lists of "women of achievement." These knew her best for her passion for Truth; her eloquent insistence on cogent proof; her scorn for stupidity and intellectual bluff in high places; and her mastery of the artful techniques of scientific research and report.

These apparently conflicting interests were really integrated expressions of her versatile personality. To those who knew her intimately through many phases of her development and activity, even these contrasting interests are but fragmentary revelations of her depth and delicacy of feeling, her liveliness of imagination, her spirited and eager enthusiasm, her fidelity of memory, her fortitude, her intellectual grasp and scope—a richness of endowment all too rare in the history of human nature.

Thus closes the story of her rich and fruitful life. I have tried to tell the story with such fidelity as I could and as objectively as possible. It is only half told, for not all of her life was occupied by childhood and professional activity. She was my college sweetheart, and then for thirty-one years my wife, but this half of the story shall remain our secret. The urge of many things I have wanted to say has usually been withheld, for these have been so intimately tied to my own emotions and evaluations that they need not be made a matter of record in such poor trappings as words. But I realize anew, in trying to cite the objective data, how much of a personality escapes the narrative when it is told by another, and how meagerly the substantial relics of a life reveal the richness of the inner spirit.

Bibliography

The following bibliography includes the books, monographs, and other publications of Leta S. Hollingworth.

Books

Functional Periodicity. Contributions to Education, No. 69. Bureau of Publications, Teachers College, Columbia University, 1914. 101 p.

The Psychology of Special Disability in Spelling. Contributions to Education, No. 88. Bureau of Publications, Teachers College, Columbia University, 1918. 105 p.

The Psychology of Subnormal Children. The Macmillan Company, 1920. 288+xix p.

Special Talents and Defects: Their Significance for Education. The Macmillan Company, 1923. 216+xix p.

Gifted Children. The Macmillan Company, 1926. 374+xxiv p.

The Psychology of the Adolescent. D. Appleton, 1928. 259+xv p. Published also by Partridge, London, 1930.

Public Addresses. The Science Press, Lancaster, Pa., 1940. 148 p.

Prairie Years. A Collection of Verse, with Photograph and brief autobiography. Columbia University Press, New York City, 1940. 35 p.

Children Above 180 I.Q. World Book Company, Yonkers, N.Y., 1942. 332+xvii p.

Articles

"The Frequency of Amentia as Related to Sex." *Medical Record,* Vol. 84, pp. 753–756, October 25, 1913. Wm. Woods & Co., New York.

"Variability as Related to Sex Differences in Achievement." *The American Journal of Sociology*, Vol. 19, pp. 510–530, January, 1914.

"An Economic and Social Study of Feeble-minded Women." *Medical Record*, Vol. 85, pp. 1025–1028, June 6, 1914. Wm. Woods & Co., New York. (With Max G. Schlapp.)

"The Comparative Variability of the Sexes at Birth." *The American Journal of Sociology*, Vol. 20, pp. 335–370, November, 1914. (With Helen Montague.)

"The Mentally Defective as Cases in the Courts of New York City." *Medical Record*, Vol. 87, pp. 337–341, February 27, 1915. Wm. Woods & Co., New York. (With Max G. Schlapp.)

"The Vocational Aptitudes of Women." Chapter X in *Vocational Psychology*, by Harry L. Hollingworth. D. Appleton, New York, 1916.

"Echolalia in Idiots: Its Meaning for Modern Theories of Imitation." *Journal of Educational Psychology*, Vol. 8, pp. 212–219, April, 1917.

"The Psychology of a Prodigious Child." *Journal of Applied Psychology*, Vol. 1, pp. 101–110, June, 1917. (With Charlotte G. Garrison and Agnes Burke.)

"Social Devices for Impelling Women to Bear and Rear Children." *American Journal of Sociology*, Vol. 22, pp. 19–29, July, 1916.

"Science and Feminism." *The Scientific Monthly*, pp. 277–284, September, 1916. (With Robert H. Lowie.)

"Phi Beta Kappa and Women Students." *School and Society*, Vol. 4, pp. 932–933, December, 1916.

"The Psychological Examination of Poor Spellers." *Teachers College Record*, Vol. 20, pp. 126–132, March, 1919.

"Special Disabilities that Contribute to Retardation in School Status." *Ungraded*, Vol. 5, pp. 49–54, December, 1919. An address delivered before the Section for Study of Retarded Children of the New York State Teachers Association, at Albany, November 24, 1919.

"Psychological Clinics in the United States." *Teachers College Record*, Vol. 22, pp. 221–225, May, 1921.

"Differential Action upon the Sexes of Forces Which Tend to Segregate the Feeble-minded." *Journal of Abnormal and Social Psychology*, Vol. 17, pp. 35–57, April–June, 1922.

"Subsequent History of E———: Five Years After the Initial Report." *Journal of Applied Psychology*, Vol. 6, pp. 205–210, June, 1922. (With Charlotte G. Garrison and Agnes Burke.)

"The Special Opportunity Class for Gifted Children: Public School 165, Manhattan." *Ungraded*, Vol. 8, pp. 121–128, March, 1923.

"The Size and Strength of Children Who Test Above 135 I.Q." *Twenty-*

Third Yearbook of the National Society for the Study of Education, Part I: *The Education of Gifted Children*, pp. 221–237. (With Grace A. Taylor.)

Experiments in the Education of the Gifted. Contributions to Education, New York Society for Experimental Education, Vol. 1, pp. 139–148. World Book Company, Yonkers, N.Y., 1924.

"Provisions for Intellectually Superior Children." Chapter XIV in *The Child, His Nature and His Needs.* Children's Foundation, 1924.

"An Introduction to Biography for Young Children Who Test Above 150 I.Q." *Teachers College Record*, Vol. 26, pp. 277–287, December, 1924.

"The Regression of Siblings of Children Who Test at or Above 135 I.Q. (Stanford-Binet)." *Journal of Educational Psychology*, Vol. 16, pp. 1–7, January, 1925. (With Margaret V. Cobb.)

"Intellectually Superior Children." *McClure's Magazine*, New Series, Vol. I, pp. 51–61, May, 1925. (Whole No. 371.)

"Development of Intelligence in the First Six Years." *Ungraded*, Vol. 10, pp. 204–207, June, 1925.

"Mental Tests in Schools." *School and Home*, Vol. 9, pp. 1–4, November, 1925.

"Vocabulary as a Symptom of Intellect." *American Speech*, Vol. 1, pp. 154–158, December, 1925.

"Getting Away from the Family: The Adolescent and His Life Plans." Chapter in *Concerning Parents: A Symposium on Modern Parenthood.* New Republic, Inc., New York, 1926.

"The Adolescent in the Family." *Child Study*, Vol. 37, pp. 5, 6, 13, January, 1926.

"Musical Sensitivity of Children Who Test above 135 I.Q. (Stanford-Binet)." *Journal of Educational Psychology*, Vol. 17, pp. 95–109, February, 1926.

"Tapping Rate of Children Who Test above 135 I.Q. (Stanford-Binet)." *Journal of Educational Psychology*, Vol. 17, pp. 505–518, November, 1926.

"Who Are Gifted Children?" *Child Study*, Vol. 5, pp. 3–5, October, 1927.

"Neuro-Muscular Capacity of Children Who Test Above 135 I.Q. (Stanford-Binet)." *Journal of Educational Psychology*, Vol. 18, pp. 88–96, February, 1927.

"Subsequent History of E———: Ten Years After the Initial Report." *Journal of Applied Psychology*, Vol. 11, pp. 385–390, October, 1927.

"The New Woman in the Making." *Current History*, Vol. 27, pp. 15–20, October, 1927.

"Helping the Nervous Child." Pamphlet published by the Lincoln School of Teachers College, 1927, 19 p.

"The Discipline of Highly Intelligent Children." *Parents' Magazine,* Vol. 3, pp. 19, 41, 42, June, 1928.

"Children Clustering at 165 I.Q. and Children Clustering at 146 I.Q. Compared for Three Years in Achievement." *Twenty-Seventh Yearbook of the National Society for the Study of Education, 1928,* Part II. *Nature and Nurture, Their Influence upon Achievement,* pp. 3–33. (With Margaret V. Cobb.)

"Psychology of the Family." *Encyclopedia Britannica,* pp. 205–206. 14th Edition, 1929.

"Summary Report on Pupils of Two Special Opportunity Classes of Very Bright Children." Pamphlet published by the Board of Education of the City of New York, October 31, 1929. 16 p.

"After High School—What?" *Parents' Magazine,* Vol. 4, pp. 21, 60, June, 1929.

"The Production of Gifted Children from the Parental Point of View." *Eugenics,* Vol. 2, pp. 3–7, October, 1929.

"Facts about Bright Children." *Babyhood,* December, 1929.

"The Child of Very Superior Intelligence as a Special Problem in Social Adjustment." *Annals of the American Academy of Political and Social Science,* 1930. Also in *Mental Hygiene,* Vol. 15, pp. 3–16, January, 1931, and in a volume, *Some Social Aspects of Mental Hygiene,* 1931, Part II, pp. 151–160, and in the *Proceedings of the First International Congress on Mental Hygiene,* 1932, pp. 47–69.

"The Systematic Error of Herring-Binet in Rating Gifted Children." *Journal of Educational Psychology,* Vol. 21, pp. 1–11, January, 1930.

"Do Intellectually Gifted Children Grow toward Mediocrity in Stature?" *Journal of Genetic Psychology,* Vol. 37, pp. 345–360, September, 1930.

"Personality Development of Special Class Children." University of Pennsylvania Bulletin, *Eighteenth Annual Schoolmen's Week Proceedings,* June 20, 1931, Vol. 31, pp. 442–446.

"Playmates for the Gifted Child." *Child Study,* Vol. 8, pp. 103–104, December, 1930.

"Juvenile Achievement as Related to Size." *Teachers College Record,* Vol. 32, pp. 236–244, December, 1930. (With Howard A. Gray.)

"Special Gifts and Special Deficiencies" and "The Adolescent Child." Chapters XX and XXIII in *Handbook of Child Psychology.* Clark University Press, Worcester, Mass., 1931.

"How Should Gifted Children Be Educated?" *Baltimore Bulletin of Education,* Vol. 50, pp. 195–198, May, 1931.

"Who Should Direct the Behavior Clinic?" An address delivered before the Board of Education of the City of New York, February 19, 1931. *The Principal*, pp. 10–12, April, 1931.

"Developmental Problems of Middle Adolescence." *Westminster Leader*, Vol. V, October, 1931.

"Late Adolescence." *Westminster Leader*, Vol. V, pp. 24–25, November, 1931.

"The Achievements of Gifted Children Enrolled and Not Enrolled in Special Opportunity Classes." *Journal of Educational Research*, Vol. 24, pp. 1–7, November, 1931. (With Howard A. Gray.)

"Adolescence: The Difficult Age." A radio address sponsored by the National Advisory Council on Radio in Education, December 19, 1931. Published by the University of Chicago Press, December, 1931. Also pp. 38–42 in "Listener's Note Book," No. 2. (Photograph.)

"How One Race Judges Another for Physical Attractiveness." *Journal of Social Psychology*, Vol. 3, pp. 463–469, November, 1932. (With R. Madden.)

"Who Is the Gifted Pupil?" University of Pennsylvania Bulletin, *Nineteenth Annual Schoolmen's Week Proceedings*, 1932, Vol. 32, pp. 239–246.

"Recognizing Gifted Children." *The League Script* (Minneapolis Teachers League), Vol. 13, pp. 7–9, December, 1932.

"Psychological Service for Public Schools." *Teachers College Record*, Vol. 34, pp. 368–379, February, 1933.

"Education." Chapter XX in *The Problem of Mental Disorder*. McGraw-Hill Book Company, New York, 1934.

"Problem Children." Chapter in *Childcraft: Teacher's Problems*, pp. 207–226. (Reprinted in *Childcraft*, Vol. 8: *Guidance of the Child*, pp. 70–89, 1939.) The Quarrie Corporation, Chicago.

"The Centile Status of Gifted Children at Maturity." *Journal of Genetic Psychology*, Vol. 45, pp. 106–120, September, 1934. (With R. M. Kaunitz.)

"Psychological Weaning." *The Red-Book*, Vol. 70, p. 120, October, 1934.

"The Comparative Beauty of the Faces of Highly Intelligent Adolescents." *Journal of Genetic Psychology*, Vol. 47, pp. 268–281, December, 1935.

"Adult Status of Highly Intelligent Children." *Journal of Genetic Psychology*, Vol. 49, pp. 215–226, September, 1936. (With Irving Lorge.)

"Binet's Contribution to Social Science." *The Consulting Psychologist*, Vol. 2, pp. 9–12, March, 1936.

"The Development of Personality in Highly Intelligent Children." *Fifteenth Yearbook of the Department of Elementary School Principals of the National Education Association, July, 1936*.

"The Terman Classes at Public School 500." *Journal of Educational Sociology*, Vol. 10, pp. 86–90, October, 1936.

"A New Deal for Ability." (Editorially changed to "Some Suggestions on Scholarships.") *The Independent Journal of Columbia University*, December 4, 1936.

"The Founding of Public School 500: Speyer School." *Teachers College Record*, Vol. 38, pp. 119–128, November, 1936.

"Bright Students Take Care of Themselves." *North American Review*, Vol. 243, pp. 261–273, June, 1937.

"The Importance of Studying Mental Deviates." (Photograph by Késslère.) *Journal of Consulting Psychology*, Vol. 1, pp. 73–75, September–October, 1937.

"Application of the Bernreuter Inventory of Personality to Highly Intelligent Adolescents." *Journal of Psychology*, Vol. 4, pp. 287–293, October, 1937. (With Metta M. Rust.)

"An Enrichment Curriculum for Rapid Learners at Public School 500: Speyer School." *Teachers College Record*, Vol. 39, pp. 296–306, January, 1938.

"The Participation of Nebraska in the Intellectual and Artistic Leadership of the Nation." *University of Nebraska Special Bulletin*. (An address delivered before the alumni of the University of Nebraska, June 6, 1938, on receiving the LL.D.)

"What We Know about the Early Selection and Training of Leaders." *Teachers College Record*, Vol. 40, pp. 575–592, April, 1939. (An address delivered before the Fifth Advanced School Conference on Educational Policies, November 11, 1938.)

"Problems of Relationship between Elementary and Secondary Schools in the Case of Highly Intelligent Pupils." (An address delivered before the National Committee on Co-ordination in Secondary Education at a Symposium on "The Education of Pupils of High Intelligence." Cleveland, February 27, 1939.) *Journal of Educational Sociology*, Vol. 13, pp. 90–102, October, 1939.

The following articles were published in *The Thirty-Ninth Yearbook of the National Society for the Study of Education: Intelligence, Its Nature and Nurture*, 1940. Part I: *Comparative and Critical Exposition*; Part II: *Original Studies and Experiments*.

"The Significance of Deviates." Part I, pp. 43–66.

"The Problem of Comparing Races." Part I, pp. 257–261.

"Intelligence as an Element in Personality." Part I, pp. 271–275.

"Personal Reactions to the Thirty-Ninth Yearbook." Part I, pp. 451–454.

"The Course of Mental Development in Slow Learners under an 'Experience' Curriculum." Part II, pp. 245–254. (With Pritchard and Horan.)

In addition to the foregoing, there are numerous *Reviews* of the books and monographs of others, *Summaries* of literature in special fields, *Memoranda* to deliberative assemblies and conferences or commissions, *Reports* to the Dean of Teachers College, *Reports* to the Board of Superintendents, and unsigned *Contributions* to the reports of committees organizing *Yearbooks, Programs,* and *Surveys.*

The following bibliography includes the books, monographs, and other publications **about** Leta S. Hollingworth.*

Teachers College Record. (1940, December). *42* (3). Special issue containing articles written by Leta Hollingworth's students on the six major fields in which she had worked. Introductions to the volume were written by Arthur I. Gates and by Harry Hollingworth.
    Spencer, D. Clinical psychology and mental adjustments, pp. 196–205.
    Green, K. B. The social and professional status of women, pp. 206–209.
    Carroll, H. A. Intellectually gifted children, pp. 212–227.
    Pritchard, M.C. The psychology and education of subnormal children, pp. 228–238.
    Russell, D. H. Trends and needs in the study of special abilities and disabilities, pp. 239–249.
    Washburne, J.N. Interpretation of adolescent psychology and needs, pp. 250–264.
Roeper Review. (1990, March). *12* (3). Special issue containing the proceedings of the Hollingworth Commemorative Conference, University of Nebraska-Lincoln, October 1989.
    Roweton, W. E. Leta Hollingworth: A personal profile of Nebraska's pioneering psychologist, pp. 136–141.
    Miller, R. Leta Stetter Hollingworth: Pioneer woman of psychology, pp. 142–145.
    Benjamin, L. T. Jr., Leta Stetter Hollingworth: Psychologist, educator, feminist, pp. 145–151.

*This bibliography is added to this reprinted edition of the biography.

Shields, S. A. "Ms. Pilgrim's progress" and commentary, pp.151–156.

Fagan, T. K. Contributions of Leta Hollingworth to school psychology, pp.157–161.

Borland, J. H. An equal among firsts: Leta Hollingworth's contributions to the psychology and education of the gifted, pp.162–166.

Stanley, J. C. Leta Hollingworth's contributions to above-level testing of the gifted, pp.166–171.

Silverman, L. K. Social and emotional development of the gifted: The discoveries of Leta Hollingworth, pp.171–178.

Kerr, B. Leta Stetter Hollingworth's legacy to counseling and guidance, pp. 178–181.

Kearney, K. Leta Hollingworth's unfinished legacy: Children above 180 IQ., pp. 181–183, 186–188.

Santmire, T. E. Understanding gifted adolescents: Another legacy of Leta Stetter Hollingworth, pp.188–192.

Griffin, N. S. Six walls of the hogan: Leta Hollingworth as a model for a teacher of learning disabled gifted children, pp.192–197.

Zimmerman, E. Leta Stetter Hollingworth's contributions to the study of art talent, pp.198–202.

Tolan, S. S. From production to nurturing: Hollingworth and parental perspectives today, pp. 203–207.

Benbow, C. P. Leta Stetter Hollingworth: A pilgrim in research in her time and ours, pp. 210–215.

Harris, C. R. The Hollingworth longitudinal study: Follow-up, findings, and implications, pp. 216–222.

Piechowski, M. M. The heart of Leta S. Hollingworth, pp. 228–235.

Benjamin, L. T., Jr. (1975). The pioneering work of Leta Hollingworth in the psychology of women. *Nebraska History, 56,* 493–505.

Benjamin, L. T., Jr. (1988, August). Caffeine and Coca-Cola: Leta Hollingworth's ticket to graduate school. In W. E. Roweton (Chair), *Leta Stetter Hollingworth: Her life and times.* Symposium conducted at the meeting of the American Psychological Association, Atlanta, GA.

Benjamin, L. T., Jr., & Shields, S. A. (in press). Leta Stetter Hollingworth (1886–1939). In A. N. O'Connell & N. F. Russo (Eds.), *Women in psychology.* Westport, CT: Greenwood Press.

Dorr, R. C. (1915, September 19). Is woman biologically barred from success? *New York Times Magazine,* pp. 15–16.

Peavey, L. S., & Smith, U. (1983). Leta Stetter Hollingworth—An experimental life (pp. 79–99). *Women who change things.* New York: Scribners.

Poffenberger, A. T. (1940). Leta Stetter Hollingworth: 1886–1939. *American Journal of Psychology, 53,* 299–301.

Pritchard, M. C. (1951). The contributions of Leta S. Hollingworth to the study of gifted children. In P. Witty (Ed.), *The gifted child,* Chapter 4 (pp. 47–85). Boston: D. C. Heath.

Roemele, V. S. (1971). Leta Anna Stetter Hollingworth. In *Notable American women, 1607–1950.* E. T. James (Ed.). Cambridge, MA: Harvard University Press.

Rosenberg, R. (1984). Leta Hollingworth: Toward a sexless intelligence. In M. Lewin (Ed.), *In the shadow of the past: Psychology portrays the sexes* (pp. 77–96). New York: Columbia University Press.

Roweton, W. E. (1987). *Leta Stetter Hollingworth: Her childhood years in northwest Nebraska.* Unpublished manuscript.

Shields, S. A. (1975). Ms. pilgrim's progress: The contributions of Leta Stetter Hollingworth to the psychology of women. *American Psychologist, 30,* 852–857.

Shields, S. A. (1982). The variability hypothesis. *Signs, 7,* 769–797.

Shields, S. A. (in press). Leta Stetter Hollingworth and the study of individual differences. In G. A. Kimble, M. Wertheimer, & C. L. White (Eds.), *Pioneers in psychology.* Hillsdale, NJ: Lawrence Erlbaum Associates.

Shields, S. A., & Mallory, M. E. (1987). Leta Stetter Hollingworth speaks on "Columbia's Legacy." *Psychology of Women Quarterly, 11,* 285–300.

Silverman, L. K. (1989). It all began with Leta Hollingworth: The story of giftedness in women. *Journal for the Education of the Gifted, 12,* 86–98.

Silverman, L. K. (1989). The legacy of Leta Hollingworth. *Gifted Child Quarterly, 33,* 123–124.

Terman, L. M. (1944). Review of *Leta Stetter Hollingworth: A biography. Journal of Applied Psychology, 28,* 357–359.

White, W. L., & Renzulli, J. S. (1987). A forty year follow-up of students who attended Leta Hollingworth's school for gifted students. *Roeper Review, 10,* 89–94.

Zimmerman, E. (1985). To test all things: The life and work of Leta Stetter Hollingworth. In M. A. Stankiewicz & E. Zimmerman (Eds.), *Women art educators II* (pp. 64–81). Bloomington, IN: Indiana University Press.

Zimmerman, E. (1987). Art talent and research in the 1920s and 1930s: Norman C. Meier's and Leta Stetter Hollingworth's theories about special abilities. In G. Clark, E. Zimmerman, & M. Zurmuehlen (Eds.), *Understanding art testing: Past influences, Norman C. Meier's contributions, present concerns, and future possibilities* (pp. 36–45). Reston, VA: National Art Education Assn.